MW01116301

Liberal Arts Education
and College Architecture
in Steamboat Springs

A Personal History

Cover photo:
A postcard view of Steamboat Springs with the Lincoln Jones' designed college buildings overlooking the town from the vantage point of Woodchuck Hill. These buildings stood sentry over Steamboat Springs for nearly fifty years and were recently removed from the hillside campus.
Photo by Bob McConnell. Courtesy of Tread of Pioneers Museum, Steamboat Springs, Colorado.

Back cover photos:
Bristol Hall before and after.
Built in 1993, Bristol Hall's architects, AndersonMasonDale, planned the building's color scheme with a red brick facing and a yellow façade. One year later, after much community discussion, red stucco covered the concrete façade and the yellow was replaced with red.
Photos by Ken Proper.

Liberal Arts Education and College Architecture in Steamboat Springs

A Personal History

By Robert P. Baker

Neponset Publishing Company
Phippsburg, Colorado

For information and permissions:
    Email Neponset Publishing Company at NeponsetPubCo@yahoo.com

Non-fiction, history, architecture, education

ISBN: 978-0-9961366-0-0 (trade paperback)

Liberal Arts Education and College Architecture in Steamboat Springs: A Personal History
Published by Neponset Publishing Company, Phippsburg, Colorado
Written by Robert P. Baker, Phippsburg, Colorado
Edited by Susan Hoskinson, Fort Collins, Colorado
Electronic pre-press by Gail Blinde, Fort Collins, Colorado
Printed by Citizen Printing, Fort Collins, Colorado
Additional copies may be acquired from the website of *Off The Beaten Path* bookstore,
Steamboat Springs, Colorado, or SteamboatBooks.com

No one can make judgments on history
who has not experienced it in himself.

—Goethe, Maxims

Contents

Acknowledgments

The first people I should thank (although "thank" is perhaps not the right word) are the administrators of Colorado Mountain College, who made the decision in 2010 to destroy buildings on the Alpine Campus that were designed by Lincoln Jones in the 1960s, a destruction that motivated this book.

The first version of this book, during my first year of writing, was a study of Lincoln Jones, and I want to thank the architects Carl Worthington of Boulder and Robert S. Ralston of Steamboat Springs, and also Glen Jones, for their kind help in this endeavor.

The second version, during the second year of writing, expanded the book to the entire history of higher education in Steamboat Springs. For this I am indebted to George Tolles, George Bagwell, and John Vickery for their help, and also to Kevin Williams, the librarian at the Alpine Campus who helped me in many large and small ways.

The third version, during the third year of writing, was due to my good friend John Grassby, a lawyer in Steamboat Springs, but also a writer of fine fiction and a Renaissance man, who convinced me to add my personal history to the narrative.

The fourth version, during the fourth year of writing, was due to the constructive criticisms of many who graciously read the text, and to my attempts to find the right balance between the historical and the personal.

This is the fifth version in 2015,

In addition, I need to thank the librarians at the Western History Department of the Denver Public Library and the staff at the Tread of Pioneers Museum in Steamboat Springs, and all the people mentioned in the book who gave me interviews and shared their thoughts with me. Ken Proper did a fine professional photography job and also gave me his expert opinion for many aspects of this book. Karen Malcolm, the daughter of Robert Pietrowski, relived difficult memories for the sake of historical truth.

I also want to thank my wife, Susie, for her patience and forbearance as I struggled with the craft of writing.

Finally, I have to thank the two thousand or more students that I taught in Steamboat Springs, who always taught me more than I taught them. This book is for you.

Robert P. Baker

Introduction

WHEN STUDENTS GRADUATE from high school in America, they are faced with a bewildering array of hierarchical choices for post-secondary education. At the top are the elite, private four-year schools—Harvard, Yale, Princeton, Stanford—reserved for the wealthy and the meritorious. Below these schools are smaller private and sometimes religious four-year colleges. There are state universities, in some states divided into one university that emphasizes more academic courses and another land-grant university that focuses more on agriculture, forestry, and engineering. Below the four-year schools are two-year schools, divided into private junior colleges and local community colleges supported by tax dollars. The community colleges in America have always had a strong vocational outlook, but many also provide "lower-division" (freshmen and sophomore) survey courses that transfer to four-year schools. In addition to all this, there are private technical colleges and universities that advertise heavily on television and provide mostly computer online courses in a number of technical or business areas.

There was a time when the elite four-year colleges, small private colleges, and even some community colleges combined cognitive learning with the moral idea of building an integrated self.[1] This was the American liberal arts tradition of higher education, an education that combined learning with the nonmarketable but personally important idea of human flourishing. This moral imperative was conveyed through classes in philosophy, the classics, history, the fine arts, drama, poetry, literature, and the visual arts. These courses, while not directly useful in terms of making a living, " . . . fostered a form of reflective self-cultivation that can and ought to be a continuous life activity."[2] Because these courses were a large part of higher education, specialists in these disciplines could count on a university or college teaching career. It is now safe to generalize that in the first decades of the twenty-first century higher education in all its manifestations has tilted toward a "consumerist and careerist monoculture," to the point where the majority of young people entering college have no idea that something called a liberal arts education ever existed.[3] They will never be introduced to it, and its full-time teachers are slowly disappearing from the higher education scene.[4]

In this book the microcosm, the history of higher education in Steamboat Springs, Colorado, is reflective of the macrocosm, the larger educational history of America. This book tells the story of the rise of liberal arts education in Steamboat Springs before the coming of Colorado Mountain College (CMC), the continuation of that kind of education after the coming of CMC in the 1980s and 1990s, and the diminution of that tradition in the twentieth-first century. It may surprise some readers that this story is combined with a study of architecture on that campus, and in the first chapter I will try to convince my readers that a certain kind of architectural aesthetics is a necessary component of the liberal arts.

Out of the welter of higher educational possibilities and after some strange peregrinations at various levels, I became a teacher at the Steamboat Springs Campus of Colorado Mountain College. My personal history as a college teacher is intimately intertwined with the liberal arts and requires me to write about my own journey and about the small world in which I taught. The chapters on higher education in Steamboat Springs before I arrived are by necessity written as from a distance, but the rest of the book combines the personal with the factual.

When I was trained as a historian in graduate school, I was encouraged to write history both as an interesting narrative and as objectively as possible—in the third person "god's eye" view.

This book presents a very different kind of history, still, I hope, an interesting narrative, but written from both my personal passion for the liberal arts and also my grieving for its demise. This approach walks the "razor's edge" between the subjective and the objective and is not without some degree of discomfort and doubt. Have I imagined a "reality" that was not really there or imposed my biases on the past? All I can plead is that I have been as honest as possible in revealing my beliefs, and the reader will have to decide if I have judged fairly or unfairly.

The juxtaposition of architecture, higher education, and changing modes of being in the world did not arise in me fully explained and understood, as from the head of Zeus. The famous quote of Nietzsche comes to mind: "After we have finished building our house, we notice that we have inadvertently learned something in the process, something that we absolutely should have known before we—began to build."[5] However, as you will see, the epiphany of understanding in my case was caused not by the construction of a building but by the destruction of one.

American Liberal
Arts Education

AMERICAN HISTORIAN DANIEL J. BOORSTIN has written, "The discord between man as maker and man as thinker has accounted for much of the restlessness in American political and intellectual life."[1] The founding of the University of Virginia in 1817 by Thomas Jefferson reflected the tension between man as maker and man as thinker. Jefferson's concern, because America was engaged in subduing an unruly nature, was overwhelmingly practical. The curriculum of Jefferson's University of Virginia featured vocational classes in agriculture, medicine, and commerce, but also included nonpractical philosophy, history, ethics, and the fine arts courses.[2] Other institutions of higher education in America were originally religious, usually in the Protestant tradition, such as Harvard, founded in 1636. They also reflected the tension between vocational and nonvocational, because the founders of the religious colleges wanted schools of higher education to produce preachers, but also included classes in general education. What united the Enlightenment vision of men like Jefferson and the religious educators was a strong vertical attraction toward an ideal of a nonaristocratic vision of the noble life that was to show the world the uniqueness of America.

As the country moved westward and more colleges and universities were established, a liberal arts education became defined as one that would produce a well-rounded person both intellectually and morally, a free citizen who would take an active part in civic life.[3] This education would also challenge the student to think about his life outside of the market economy. Anthony Knonman has written, "Once upon a time, and not all that long ago, many college teachers, especially in the humanities, believed they had a responsibility to lead their students in an organized examination of this question of what living is for." Education that was not "useful" was the genius of liberal arts education.

> It is the non-vocational, non-career-based 'uselessness' of the subject matter that opens the door to appreciating knowing for the sake of knowing and that drives home the fact that learning is of value in and of itself, without regard to whether it is directly linked to a marketable skill.[4]

The educational models for liberal education were small colleges such as Antioch, Haverford, St. John's, Wesleyan, and Reed, and some larger universities such as Columbia, Harvard, and the University of Chicago. The curriculum usually emphasized literature, foreign languages, art, music, history, mathematics, psychology, and science.

Until the 1960s the dominant model for higher education in America looked something like this: during the first two years of college a student would take a broad range of courses in order to taste the spectrum of intellectual life, and he or she would begin to grasp critical thinking and the importance of interpretations at an intellectual level above that taught in high school. During these years the student would discover the love of learning. In the last two years of college the student would choose a major subject and begin to make his or her own interpretations. Then one would go on to graduate school to become a professional in one's chosen field. This was a pre-modern scheme, much like the medieval craft guilds where one began as an apprentice, moved up to journeyman, and ended as a master craftsman.[5]

The first two years of college were the most important years of a person's life. It was during those years that the young student was encouraged to imagine whole realms of intellectual and personal possibilities. For a short time, a "time-out" really, the student could dream of an ideal flourishing life and the actualization of one's potentialities within an ideal community of like-minded individuals. This schema reflected Protestant theology: that every individual created by God had a special "calling," and the job of education was to help the student find his or her authentic niche in society. This was a philosophy of education meant to counter the medieval word, *acedia*, defined by Kierkegaard as "the despairing refusal to be oneself."[6] For authenticity to emerge, the student had to relinquish the idea of intellectual activity as work, and instead see it as a kind of effortless possession that was accompanied by leisure, not in the form of idleness but as contemplation. In contrast to today, when students from the time of kindergarten are taught through testing that school is difficult toil and trouble, the student in liberal arts was taught that knowledge was a gift that comes through deep play, that there was a ludic joy to the real intellectual world.

For a short period of one's life, during the most important formative years, from ages eighteen to twenty-one, liberal arts was pursued as an education that pretended "as if" the practical world did not exist. Students were counseled, "Don't think about what you want to major in until the end of your sophomore year."[7] College would be the locale where young people would " . . . find help in navigating the territory between adolescence and adulthood."[8] The locale was important: a university or college campus became an integral aspect of the liberal arts. A utopian architecture, set within an idealized natural environment that looked back to a time that never was, was at the heart of a liberal arts education.

Despite the possible counter-examples of Oxford and Cambridge, the idea of a "campus" that featured a welcoming natural environment, was rarely found in Europe.[9] An important initiator of the ideal campus was Thomas Jefferson, who set an important example with the University of Virginia:

> Jefferson believed that architecture was the heart of the American cause. In his mind, a building was not merely a walled structure, but a metaphor for American ideology. . . The University of Virginia was to become the physical model of Jefferson's cultural and educational ideals.[10]

Jefferson's University of Virginia united living and learning with buildings for students and faculty organized around an open space of lawn to facilitate dialogue. Designed for order, simplicity, and centrality, it was Jefferson's hope that "from architecture would flow education in taste, values, and ideals."[11]

The American university campus symbolized, at a deeper level, a kind of religiosity. From neolithic times, five to six thousand years ago, human beings built structures—stone enclosures—that set apart a sacred space, a piece of the earth that served to remind them of a golden or utopian age that no longer existed.[12] Later, organized religions transformed this vision into the ideal of a heavenly afterlife, and churches and temples were built on sacred space. During the European Enlightenment of the eighteenth century, this vision was secularized.[13] Jefferson's neoclassical architecture harked back to that imagined period of Greek history when Socrates and Plato inaugurated the dialogue, and Aristotle wrote of a flourishing life.[14] That classical Greek world never really existed in this idealized form, but through the use of imaginative architecture one could pretend "as if" this ideal education of the past could continue into the future on the sacred space of the college or university campus.

The campus in higher education was wedded to a utopian ideal of nature as beautiful and uplifting; nature was "picturesque."[15] This view of nature extended back to the Greek Stoics and forward to the Enlightenment. For Thomas Jefferson, nature was a "work of art" crafted by the Master Craftsman to contain an "inmost order and stability."[16] He believed that the large plan of nature made necessary every plant and animal, and like his contemporaries, believed himself as a link in the great chain of being extending from the lowest forms of life to the highest, the human being.[17] Jefferson's beliefs set the tone for liberal arts campuses in America. In a natural setting with the appropriate architecture, the ontological authority of nature would encourage both students and faculty to relax, use their imaginations, destroy demon time, and enjoy the adventure of learning.

In the 1950s the launch of Sputnik convinced many Americans that their country had fallen behind the Russians in science and technology, and there ensued a lively discussion over the means and ends of higher education. A debate occurred between Mortimer Adler of the University of Chicago and James Conant of Harvard. Adler, who had pioneered liberal arts education, argued for the traditional liberal arts education; Conant responded that America should scrap humanism and concentrate on science and technology.[18] The issue was clearly defined: should higher education be "liberal" or "servile."[19] The antagonism between pragmatic education and nonmarketable education and the discord between man as thinker and man as maker was to be played out in higher education during the next half-century.

An Apprenticeship in Liberal Arts Education

BORN IN 1939, I grew up before the advent of "middle" schools, and my first school, Bret Harte Elementary School on the south side of Chicago, spanned kindergarten to eighth grade. In my mind the school was like a beautiful little castle, with fortress-like decorations on the roof and large, south-facing windows overlooking Stony Island Avenue. Its small classrooms contained not more than 250 children, and students in the higher grades were required to care for the younger students, by helping small children across the street as patrol boys, taking off and putting on their winter coats, and keeping order at recess. I began kindergarten on the first floor and finished eighth grade on the second. I lived two blocks away and walked to school every day.

By the autumn of 1953, I was a student at Hyde Park High School at 63rd Street and Stony Island Avenue. Hyde Park High School was a rectangular, four-story building with a classical façade.[1] It was jail-like and gloomy on the inside, and I often thought that it resembled a prison.[2] I was not particularly happy there. Lonely and alienated, I read the gritty writers of the Chicago school—Nelson Algren and James T. Farrell—and listened to the jazz of Charlie Parker and Thelonious Monk. The 1955 movie *Rebel Without a Cause* and the actor James Dean perfectly

11

reflected my mood. I grew my hair long with a "DA" and wore shirts with "Mr. B" collars and peg-legged pants.[3] A wonderful teacher, Ms. Sadie Friedlander, suggested that I read Schopenhauer. Was it true that human beings were fated to endure a life of pain? I tried to wrap my mind around that question.

The saving grace of my life was the natural setting of the Hyde Park neighborhood with tree-lined streets and Jackson Park with sunken garden and Japanese pagodas.[4] Hyde Park was also home of the University of Chicago.[5] During my high-school years I often went to the William Rainey Harper Library, warm and welcoming yet dark and strange. It had been designed in the 1920s by the architectural firm of Shepley, Rutan, & Coolidge. I wandered into Rockefeller Memorial Church, a massive neo-Gothic structure, and I "audited" (actually just snuck into) philosophy and history classes in the famous Cobb Hall on the Quadrangle.

In the early 1950s a university campus was more than just its buildings; the Hyde Park neighborhood, on 55th and 57th streets, was characterized by small shops, bookstores, and coffee houses, and, of course, taverns and bars. I remember in particular VanTellington's used bookstore in an old 1893 world's fair building on 57th Street where I spent many hours looking at books and talking with the owner.

In 1951 *Catcher in the Rye* was published, and at some point during my high-school years I read it and became very Holden Caulfieldish. I drank a lot of beer and tried, unsuccessfully, to "make it" with the girls in my class. Life in Chicago somehow seemed very wrong in ways I could and could not identify. I was an intolerable, sneering, cynical, immature teenager. My father, a successful alumnus of Knox College in Galesburg, Illinois, was able to get me enrolled into Knox, and off I went. My experiences there changed me both as a person and as a student. It inculcated in me a lifelong appreciation of a liberal arts education.

George Washington Gale founded Knox College in the nineteenth century. He was deeply influenced by the liberal arts tradition, and in Galesburg he wanted to imitate the University of Virginia.[6] The campus, on a flat piece of land south of Main Street, was by the 1950s characterized by four buildings facing each other across a vast expanse of grass. The dominant building was Old Main, built in 1857. It was a strange, uncanny structure almost impossible to characterize; idiosyncratic neo-Gothic would probably be the most accurate description. It was designed by a Swedish immigrant architect named Charles Ulricson and it was not original: Ulricson used the Chapel in the Sky (1834-1837) at the University of the City of New York and the Wadsworth Atheneum in Hartford, Connecticut, as his sources. But in defiance of the sympathies of the Knox trustees, he loaded the building with secret Masonic symbolism that gave the building its strangeness.[7] As a student in the 1950s I was not aware of the Masonic touches—just of the slightly bizarre nature of the building.

Facing Old Main across the expanse of grass was the library, a neo-Gothic, white stone building built in 1928, designed by Shepley, Rutan, & Coolidge, the same architects who designed the Harper Library at the University of Chicago. In fact, it was a miniature version of that library. At right angles to Old Main and the library, also facing each other, were red-brick structures: Alumni Hall, built in 1890 in a style called Richardsonian Romanesque that emphasized semi-circular arches and deep windows, designed by Elijah E. Myers, who also designed the state capitol buildings of Texas and Colorado. Directly opposite was a nondescript cafeteria and dorm called Seymour Hall. These four buildings, facing and at right angles, were the central hub of the campus. Beautiful oak, maple, and gingko trees graced the lawns, and the similarity to the University of Chicago campus made me feel at home. A science building, gym, and more dormitories away from the main quadrangle completed the campus that greeted me in 1956.

I entered Knox College woefully unprepared for college-level work, deficient in math and science, widely read in a haphazard and undisciplined manner. My turning point at Knox came in a political theory seminar given by Phil Herring, a Harvard-trained former stockbroker who somehow ended up teaching at Knox. I wrote what I considered a great paper about *The Ancient City* by Fustel de Coulanges, although I did not put much time in on it. Herring gave me an "F" and said it was nonsense, which made me really think about ideas for the first time—I ended up getting an "A" in the course. About that time, Daniel Wen Ye Kwok from Yale came to Knox to teach Chinese history, and I spent hours with him talking about Eastern ideas and philosophy. His parents had been Chinese diplomats. One day in the "Gizmo," the Knox coffeehouse located in the basement of Alumni Hall, we were talking about Mao's communism. Professor Kwok looked away and said softly, "It would be so nice to be able some day to sit by the Yangtze River, leisurely sip tea, and talk."

In the fall of 1957 I was sitting in a small, semidark room on the second floor of Old Main with seven other students in front of Professor Sam Moon. We were supposed to have read James Joyce's story "Clay" from *The Dubliners*. It was Halloween party time on the Knox campus, and I had a throbbing headache. None of us had bothered to spend much time on "Clay" or to look up the missed final verse of Maria's song, or even to wonder why she looked like a witch. Sam Moon put his hands up to his thin, expressive face, took off his glasses, and rubbed his temples. His eyes telegraphed an almost unbearable sadness as he tried to explain the meaning of Maria choosing the plate of clay. I understood immediately that Professor Moon's sadness was both a response to Joyce's story and to the inertial obtuseness of us, his students. It was precisely at that point in time that I realized I wanted to become a teacher.

I graduated from Knox College in the spring of 1960 with an unsatisfied intellectual curiosity, a degree in history and religion, and an acceptance letter from the history department of Stanford University. In July of 1960 I pushed my little French car—a Simca Aronde—west. This was the era before the interstate highways were finished, and I drove U.S. Highway 6 & 40 out of Denver and finally chugged over Rabbit Ears Pass into Steamboat Springs. I remember it as a little mountain town that quickly passed. I knew nothing of what my future would hold or that I would spend the majority of my life in Colorado's Yampa Valley. Of course I could not possibly imagine that educators in Steamboat Springs were, as I was driving through, dreaming of a liberal arts college.

Stanford, known as "the farm," is located on 7,000 acres in Palo Alto, California. In the fall of 1960, when I arrived, the campus was not as built up as it is today nor was Palo Alto the upscale town it has become.[8] One entered Stanford through Palm Drive, a mile-long road surrounded on both sides by palm trees and live oaks, to arrive at the quadrangle. Frederick Law Olmsted, who designed Jackson Park in Chicago, also designed the Stanford campus. The architectural style was a combination of Richardsonian Romanesque with its semicircular arches, and California Mission with a courtyard, arched corridors, and red-roofed adobe buildings. The architects were the same group who designed buildings at the University of Chicago and Knox College—Shepley, Rutan, & Coolidge.[9] I lived in student housing in Menlo Park, three miles away, rode my bicycle every morning along Palm Drive, walked the corridors to the student union and the library, and felt very much at home.

When I arrived at Stanford in 1960, History Corner had not yet been remodeled, nor had the history department itself, although both "remodelings" would occur during my tenure there. Initially, the atmosphere in the department was rather relaxed; one had the feeling that you had joined an exclusive club of like-minded intellectuals who viewed the study of history as a part of the humanities, a branch of literature. The mood changed in 1962 when Gordon Craig, a well-known German historian from Princeton University, was hired to beef up the research faculty and weed out the graduate students. His first act was to flunk a friend of mine on his doctoral exam, an act that was calculated to and actually did strike terror into the souls of the graduate students. I was fortunate enough to have as an adviser and protector one of the "old guard" faculty members, David Harris, a gentleman scholar, widely read, deeply educated, and interested in teaching. Every year he would bring his wife, Christina Phelps Harris, to monitor his classes. I asked him why. Because, he said, "Teaching is a craft, and often you get into bad habits and don't realize it, and my wife points them out to me."[10]

In my second year Professor Harris allowed me a one-on-one tutorial reading about the French Revolution. He said to me, "Don't read anything until you have a question in your mind that needs to be answered by the material." The question I asked was: Why were the French revolutionaries, successful when they carried out a political revolution, unsuccessful when they tried to impose a cultural revolution that would overturn French society, even changing the days of the week and the months of the year? Each French historian I read gave a different answer. But the method stuck with me when I began teaching. It was not enough to throw a history textbook in front of a student and command, "learn this." You have to stimulate in that student's mind some reason to read the material, some question that needs to be answered.

In another seminar on American diplomatic history, I encountered Thomas A. Bailey, dean of American historians. Bailey was a consummate storyteller. History for him was a fascinating narrative that would hold one's attention as much as any fictional tale. Every historian tells a story. It is a discipline of competing narratives.

In 1963 I received a French governmental fellowship and lived in northern France for a year. I returned to California in the fall of 1964 and bicycled to the Stanford Mall. Across the street in a small park a band was playing. Kids slightly younger than I were dancing and wearing very bright clothing, or very little clothing at all. It was a "Be-In." I was astounded. Some cultural sea change had occurred while I was in Europe. It appeared that a significant number of young people believed American consumer society was lacking some essential quality, and if the society would not change, the young people would change themselves. It was the beginning of years of protest, by youths, Native Americans, African-Americans, anti-war protestors, and women.[11]

In 1964 I began to teach the western civilization course at Stanford. Western civilization at that time was taught by a small group of young scholars who were either writing their theses or preparing them for publication; our adviser was Paul Seaver, a Renaissance scholar who was also interested in teaching excellence. I taught three sections in the basement rooms of History Corner. It was there that I found my calling. I was not going to be a great scholar or a star in the intellectual world, but I could try to be a great teacher to freshmen and sophomores who were beginning to understand what it meant to be a critical thinker.

I learned something even more important about teaching at Stanford. The course of western civilization encompassed history, literature, philosophy, art, and music; it was the essence of a beginning liberal arts education. As social ferment arose among our students, those of us teaching "civ" spent countless hours in a seminar room on the first floor of History Corner trying to imagine a teaching of history that would change with the times. We were especially concerned with feminism, racism, and the Third World.

Among the twelve or so instructors, we were allowed to write our own syllabi and choose our own readings. My students were very critical of many of my opinions and my readings, and I encouraged their criticisms. Over a four-year period, I learned that the best teaching comes when students believe that they have some control over what goes on in the classroom, that the teacher is also a learner, and that everyone in the room contributes to the learning experience. In a small class—our sections were limited to twenty students—dialogue between students and the teacher created an excitement that led to a love of reading and learning. I was learning as much from the students as I was teaching them, an appropriate pedagogy for the first two years of college. It really did not matter if we covered all of the material; what was important was the level of excitement in the classroom.

In 1968 my four-year contract teaching western civilization at Stanford ended. I had a doctorate but was without a job. At the last minute a professor of European history at Colorado State University (CSU) in Fort Collins resigned, and due to some old-boy Stanford connections I was offered a teaching position. Colorado was to be my home for the rest of my life.

It would have been helpful if my professors at Stanford had said to me in 1968: In your life so far you have only experienced a liberal arts education, but now you are going to a vocational institution. But my favorite professor, David Harris, had retired in 1967, and I was left without anyone to offer me guidance. In my naiveté, I was totally unprepared for either Fort Collins or Colorado State University, and in return both the town and the university were unprepared for me.

17

After 1965 my physical appearance had changed: I let my hair grow out and started wearing dashikis and beads. When the little French Simca gave out, I bought a cream-colored 1962 Ford Falcon station wagon, and my wife and I painted it with psychedelic patterns. By 1968 in the Bay Area of California, neither my appearance nor my automobile attracted much attention. But when I drove into Fort Collins, a primarily Republican, agricultural, conservative town with its southern boundary at Drake Road, I knew that I was a "stranger in a strange land."[12]

My first view of the campus in Fort Collins was jolting. There was an older, nineteenth-century oval containing charming buildings and huge elm trees adjacent to another "modern" campus that had been constructed west of the oval in the late 1950s and was characterized by flat expanses of concrete with reinforced concrete structures. The buildings were a prime example of a misconceived Modernist International style. How could one define the buildings? I finally decided that the football stadium by the foothills would have made Albert Speer proud, while the newer buildings on campus would have fit right in with the Stalinist workers' housing outside Berlin.[13] A particularly ugly structure was the social science building where I was given an office and where I taught. Along with a huge lecture hall, it featured prison-like hallways and contained sterile, concrete block classrooms without windows.

Harry Rosenberg, the chairman, and three older professors managed the history department. Their politics ranged from conservative to liberal, but their "fear and loathing" of the cultural changes of the 1960s united them.[14] To my surprise, I lasted three years in Fort Collins, while the old guard and I danced an elaborate and antagonistic ballet that was at once educational, political, and cultural. History, that I had been taught was an integral part of the humanities, was here considered to be a social science, although none of the history faculty used any of the mathematical or statistical apparatus that defined social science.[15] History was considered a "service" appendage to the real mission of the university that was engineering and agriculture. Students who entered as freshmen were expected to declare a major immediately, and the "survey" courses that were required of them were taught in large lecture halls. Very little, if any, thought was given to the importance of the first college years or to the ideal that a liberal arts education was necessary for a flourishing life. Students during those first years were treated more like cattle in a feedlot than as special entities whose intellectual life needed to be nourished.

The history department accepted this state of affairs as normal, while I, who at Stanford University had come to define myself as a specialist in teaching freshmen and sophomores, rebelled against it. It was only years later, when I read Robert Pirsig's *Zen and the Art of Motorcycle Maintenance*, that I realized that I was not the only one trying to carry on a liberal arts educational tradition in a vocational institution. Pirsig was teaching at Montana State University at the same time that I was at CSU, and he was also trying to find his way into the craft of teaching and was obsessed with the idea of "quality." He later wrote, "The student's biggest problem was a slave mentality which had been built into him by years of carrot-and-whip grading, a mule mentality which said, 'If you won't whip me, I won't work.' "[16] Pirsig's method was phenomenological: encourage the students to pay attention to the smallest details such as individual bricks in a wall. The familiar then becomes strange and we begin to see the strange in the familiar.[17] The deliberate introduction of the uncanny requires the student to withdraw from everyday life and the constraints of culture and opens a path for real learning. My approach to teaching history became somewhat similar: the dull and familiar facts of the historical past that have been drilled into students' heads in elementary and high school were revised to contain a strangeness that deserves explanation.

I had been reading Elton Mayo's work on industrial relations at the Western Electric Plant in Hawthorne, Illinois, where workers responded positively to any change in the workplace because someone was paying attention to them.[18] My students resembled those alienated factory workers. I attempted a series of "happenings" to jar students out of their apathy and give them some sense of control. In 1969 I was teaching western civ in the large social science lecture hall, facing more than 200 students—like Jack Parr with a microphone. I told the students, "If you

19

just want a "C," don't come back, it's guaranteed; I just want to deal with students who are interested in learning." At one stroke half the class walked out, but with those who remained I had a remarkable educational experience. In a smaller French history class in which all the students were doing well, I passed out signed grade cards and let the students fill in the grade they thought they deserved. One day the students and I decided to redecorate with crepe paper and posters the bleak, concrete block classrooms in which we were assigned. I tried to break up larger classes into smaller groups and substitute a Socratic questioning and discussion for formal lectures.

Needless to say, the old guard was not pleased with these activities, and Chairman Rosenberg would periodically call me into his office. We were two antagonistic men, one young and one old, both of whom knew that the cultural gap between them was too wide to be bridged. I tried to explain that I was allowing all points of view to be expressed and was not trying to impose my view on society and history. The older professors were not listening. I became aware that besides educational differences, there was a subtext of political and spiritual dissonance. I was brimming with the religiosity of liberal arts optimism, the faith that evil could be eradicated from the world through education, and that a New Age of humanity was right around the corner. On the campus of Colorado State University in the late 1960s this optimism was garnished with rock and roll, open sexuality, and drugs—all anathema to the older professors.

In the years from 1968 to 1971 the tide of optimism and joy quickly receded. The war in Vietnam dragged on, Cambodia was bombed, at Kent State the National Guard killed students, music-goers were killed by thugs at Altamont, and Jim Morrison, Janis Joplin, and Jimi Hendrix all destroyed themselves with drugs and alcohol, Haight-Ashbury became a sordid mess. The election of Richard Nixon to the presidency in 1968 brought on a strong counter-revolution and the beginning of "dirty tricks" on college campuses.[19] On the Colorado State University campus, Old Main burned, and strange groups of students emerged as ultra-radical "Weathermen." By 1969 kids I had never seen before leaped to the forefront at rallies, yelling that we should fight the pigs, occupy buildings, start confrontations. The mood of Fort Collins turned paranoid and ugly.

I had by 1971 defined myself as a moderate radical, like many others fed up with business as usual in America: war, violence, racism, sexism, poverty, and the destruction of the environment. Increasingly I felt like Erasmus, trying to maintain some semblance of critical thought in a world where it was in short supply, or perhaps like Aleksandr Kerensky, who tried to stop the Russian Revolution in 1917 in its moderate phase.[20] The classical Greek concept that wrongdoing (except in cases of true mental illness) stems from ignorance was for me the absolute bedrock of an optimistic view of the future. With education, human beings could build a better world. In the post-1968 world that was darkening rapidly, this was a difficult faith to maintain. I was increasingly off-balance, both intellectually and personally. I felt like I was spinning out of control.[21]

Could I, if I had been more mature and behaved in a more conformist manner at Colorado State University, kept my job? Both Harry Rosenberg and I knew that I did not belong at CSU. At the end of every semester he would call me into his office to say, "Baker, your student evaluations are among the best in the department, but I am giving you an unsatisfactory rating." He and I both knew the game; he was preparing a paper trail for my departure. In the fall of 1971 the vote by the history department executive committee concerning my contract was tied: the four younger faculty members voted for me, the four older against me. It was the perfect generational split. According to *Robert's Rules of Order*, I was denied a contract. The old guard had prevailed. The chairman and I both recognized that during my time at CSU I had learned more about the craft of teaching and had been able to slightly change the carrot-and-stick mentality of education. Rosenberg was a dedicated teacher himself, but his higher loyalties were to the university.[22] He was under tremendous pressure from the university administration, the State Board of Agriculture that governed CSU, and the state legislature to rid the university of nonconformists. In the spring of 1971, together with Tom Wayman, a Marxist poet from the English department, I was out.[23] Sixteen years passed before I was to find another permanent teaching position.

It would be noble sounding and highly congratulatory if I were to say that I retreated to country life because, like Thoreau, I wanted to "live deliberately." But that was not the case. Between 1971 and 1976 I wandered geographically—spending two years on the Upper Peninsula of Michigan and going to a linguistic summer institute at the University of Santa Cruz in California. I taught extension classes wherever someone would give me a job. For two years I taught part-time in Sewall Hall at the University of Colorado, a living-learning educational experiment. In 1973 I spent several months in France doing research for a possible book on French history. In the departmental archives of the Nord Department, on the outskirts of the town of Lille, I looked out the window and saw a farmer plowing a field. I had worked on a farm during the summer months of my college years, and thought, I would rather be sitting outside on that Massey-Ferguson tractor than inside this stuffy library.

No matter how much one tries to hide it, psychological depression is an inevitable concomitant of losing a job. I felt like the "permanent outsider" in an America that had no place for me.[24] I had a friend who owned Arabian horses, and he thought we could make a living breeding and selling them. I jumped at the chance to find a retreat from mainstream America. We looked for land on the Western Slope of Colorado where I could manage a hay crop for the horses, and he could breed and train them. We found a suitably isolated piece of land with irrigated hay meadows thirty miles south of Steamboat Springs. In 1976 we walked into the Federal Land Bank on Lincoln Avenue in Steamboat Springs, and to our great shock and amazement the banker there said that sure, he would lend us money to buy the ranch.

Thus began my life in the foothills of the Flattop Mountains, where I still live. I would like to say that I was a successful hay rancher, but that was far from the case. To the bemusement of my neighbors, I made every rookie mistake that a farmer could make, and in agriculture, unlike other professions, your mistakes are right out there in the open for everyone to see and comment upon. In the spring I fixed fences and harrowed fields, in the summer I walked irrigation ditches twice a day, and in August rounded up a crew to bale hay. After two years my partner told me that the horse business was not his calling, so I was left alone on the ranch. In the winter, with the wind howling and the snow piling up, I loaded the occasional hay truck and read widely in philosophy, history, and ecology, understanding the contradiction of warming myself by the heat of a coal stove. I never really wanted to get into raising cattle, although it would have been more profitable. Scraping by as a hay farmer with time to read and think was good enough for me. I was and still am amazed at the hospitality of my rancher neighbors, who knew that I was a stranger to their culture and more than a bit odd from their point of view. Even the neighbor who helped himself to a bit of my water from time to time would come over to lend me a hand and give advice. Here is what I learned about rural culture, now rapidly disappearing: there is a built-in suspicion of outsiders, but if you are an insider, then you are accepted even if you are strange in some way or another. And, if you went over to a neighbor's house to ask for some advice or borrow a tool, you were expected to stay and talk for a while, not just state your business and leave. The same was true if a neighbor came over to my ranch to visit, there were always long and usually interesting conversations. One day another neighbor said to me, "You've got to watch out for Hippies, N******, and Greeks." I thought, well, I certainly fit one of those strange categories, but I realized that he was now including me in his culture.

Social control in capitalist society is clearly based on debt, when one borrows money then one's life is dedicated to paying it back. I struggled every year to pay off the Federal Land Bank and equipment loans. I was barely breaking even. By 1983 I was down to the last penny, had no health insurance or retirement fund, and was physically exhausted by the hard work. I had to go into Steamboat Springs to find a job.

In 1984 I walked into the newly established Alpine Campus of Colorado Mountain College and asked Olive Morton, dean of community education, what it would take to become an adjunct teacher. She answered: put a course in the catalog and get an eight-student enrollment. She let me introduce a course called "The Philosophy of Nature." I wandered down to the bar at the Cantina Restaurant on Lincoln Avenue and talked eight of the barstool inhabitants to sign up. My teaching career had begun again. As I entered the Alpine Campus' buildings for the first time, I was unaware of the long, historical tradition of liberal arts education in Steamboat Springs, and I would have been astounded to discover that I was to become a part of that tradition.

Yampa Valley College

WHILE I WAS A GRADUATE student at Stanford University, a determined group of women and men were forging a liberal arts tradition in the Colorado town of Steamboat Springs—a tradition that would become a strong influence on my life.

In the early 1960s Denver architect Victor Hornbein, born in 1914, was nearing the fifty-year mark and had already established himself as a designer of public and university buildings. In 1951 he designed the Frederick R. Ross Branch of the Denver Public Library, in 1952 the Denver Public Works Building, in 1955 the Aurora City Hall, in 1962 the University of Colorado School of Medicine Day Care Center, and in 1963 the Porter Library of Colorado Women's College.[1] He was about to embark on the most ambitious project of his life in Steamboat Springs.

Hornbein had been educated at the Denver Beaux Arts Institute of Design, a branch of the same institute in New York City. Influenced by Frank Lloyd Wright, in the 1930s Hornbein visited Oak Park, Illinois, to see Wright's buildings and tried to work at Taliesin West with the master himself. However, World War II intervened and after the war Hornbein established a practice in Denver.

Victor Hornbein in 1966.
Courtesy of Western History Collection,
Denver Public Library.

After his death in 1995, *Denver Post* architectural critic Joanne Ditmer noted:

> Throughout his career Hornbein maintained a strict modernist design ethos. He embraced: simplicity of design; limitation of rooms and spaces to that which was necessary; exclusion of unnecessary ornament; the use of natural color and natural finishes; aesthetic exploitation of the inherent nature of the materials used; a well defined relationship of inside spaces to the outside, and the whole site; and the use of an open [free] floor plan.[2]

In 1963-1964 Hornbein became involved in educational architecture and more than just architecture in the small mountain community of Steamboat Springs. The northwest Colorado town in Routt County was isolated and difficult to access, even though a year-round highway had been built over Rabbit Ears Pass. Coal mining and ranching were the dominant economic activities. The economic growth of the 1950s and early 1960s had not yet reached into the mountains.[3] Merchants in the town were desperate for some kind of economic growth, and they looked to the emerging prosperity of the rest of the United States with longing.

Lucy Bogue in 1984.
Courtesy of *Steamboat Today* Photo
Archives. Digitized by Ken Proper.

Hornbein's involvement with Steamboat Springs started with his friendship with a remarkable woman named Lucy Bogue, although how that friendship began is not known. Bogue, born Lucile Maxfield in 1911, grew up on a ranch near Carbondale in Garfield County, Colorado. Small and birdlike, she was typical of children raised with the backbreaking work on a ranch: hard-working, focused, and determined to find success somewhere.

Bogue graduated from Garfield High School in 1930. She had a family tradition of education. Her daughter, Bonnie Bogue, recounted how, "In the 1880's one of her grandfathers walked from Iowa to Leadville to become the first superintendent of schools in the silver rush towns of Leadville and Aspen."[4] Bogue first went to Colorado College, a liberal arts school in Colorado Springs, for an associate degree, and then to Colorado State College of Education (now University of Northern Colorado) in Greeley, and received a bachelor's degree in education. She married Arthur Bogue in 1935 and became a schoolteacher, wrote poetry and plays, and in Steamboat Springs looked for new outlets in which to express her energy.[5]

Lucy Maxfield Bogue was a teacher before she came to Steamboat Springs, and she took up that occupation in the public school system after she arrived. Her college education, liberal arts in Colorado Springs and vocational training in Greeley, reflected both influences. As a teacher in Steamboat Springs, Bogue developed the idea that education, and particularly higher education, was the answer to the town's economic problems. She first went in a vocational direction and tried to organize a junior college in northwest Colorado, to include five counties. She toured the area giving speeches on the "twelve reasons why a tax-supported junior college would be a benefit."[6] The project failed because every county wanted the college to be located in one of their towns and not somewhere else, and because the hard-strapped locals were against any kind of new taxes.

Bogue changed her focus for higher education after taking a job at the newly established Lowell Whiteman School in Strawberry Park, just outside Steamboat Springs. Lowell Whiteman grew up in Hayden, Colorado, west of Steamboat Springs, worked in radio and theater in Los Angeles, and then came back to start a summer camp on family land in Strawberry Park that he turned into a permanent school in 1957. Whiteman's educational ideas were formed by his friendship with Charlotte Perry and Portia Mansfield, who founded the Perry-Mansfield School of Theater and Dance in Strawberry Park in 1915.

Perry was born in 1895 and Mansfield in 1887, and they met as students at Smith College in Northampton, Massachusetts. Perry's father founded the Moffat Coal Company in Oak Creek, Colorado, south of Steamboat Springs, and also made a fortune in railroad construction. It was his money that supported the school. The Perry-Mansfield school became well known in America for its summer programs of modern dance and theater, attracting dancers Merce Cunningham and Agnes de Mille as staff members. De Mille danced at a hoedown with the local cowboys that influenced her ballet, "Rodeo." By the 1950s Perry and Mansfield had moved to Carmel, California, but they returned to Steamboat Springs every summer for their school.[7]

Charlotte Perry received a master's degree in theater from New York University in 1954, and Portia Mansfield earned a doctorate from the same school. They taught at Hunter College, the Art Institute of Chicago, and the Santa Catalina School in Monterey, California. In the late 1950s with the arrival of Lowell Whiteman's school, their influence turned Strawberry Park into the intellectual center of Routt County, and the two women became mentors for the teachers who gathered there. They brought to Routt County the message of liberal arts education influenced by modernist art, dance, and theater.

Many of the teachers in Strawberry Park were of that generation, born in the early 1930s, who emerged from World War II with an idealistic world vision. In 1949 Reinhold Niebuhr emphasized the new world of unified mankind in his book, *Faith and History*, and this theme resonated with many educated men and women.[8] In contrast to Europe, American educators still clung to the optimistic view that reasonable people, if educated well, could build a better world.[9]

Economist Alice Rivlin expressed their sentiments well in a 2012 radio interview when asked why she went into public service. Rivlin responded:

> I think that part of it comes from having been a teenager in World War Two and in the college generation of the post-war years, which was very idealistic, we wanted to make sure that there wasn't another war, we were very interested in things like world government, world federalism . . . my generation really wanted to insure world peace and prosperity and thought we could.[10]

Bogue, in her book, *Miracle on a Mountain*, described sitting at the home of Mansfield and Perry "listening to classical music and watching the golden aspen leaves come down" and experiencing the vision of a four-year liberal arts college.[11] Steamboat Springs would become a New Athens, combining the mind and body with an education that made world citizens out of Americans. The college would educate " . . . young people not only for a full rich life as Americans, but also for the greater and more challenging job of world citizenship." It would be based " . . . upon a belief in the inherent worth of each student as a personality, as opposed to the modern trend of relegating him to a print-card number."[12] Bogue went further. She wanted only well-behaved and well-dressed students for her college that would promote "the ethical standards which so many of America's young people are seeking today."[13] Bogue incorporated the Yampa Valley College (YVC) in 1962 and optimistically hoped to raise $2,450,000 for her new college.[14]

In these enthusiastic times anything seemed possible. In the early 1960s there were more students than colleges to hold them. Between 1963 and 1975 the total number of universities and colleges doubled, and students in higher education rose from 2.7 million in 1955 to more than 7 million by the end of the 1960s.[15]

For one woman to found a college was a formidable undertaking but Bogue's husband was a well-respected banker in the community, and the merchants and ranchers of Steamboat Springs and Routt County, even if they did not share her vision of education, were willing to support any venture that might bring money and business into the area. She was an indefatigable recruiter and traveled widely to find students for the new college, even though it was new and not accredited.

The college started in 1962 with eleven full-time and thirty-six part-time students. By 1963-1964 the student population had grown to 150. The first students were not only from Steamboat Springs and other states, but also came from Kenya, Japan, and Central and South America. This reflected the international influence of the Strawberry Park educators and the fact that Bogue gave full scholarships to all foreign students. The first brochure for Yampa Valley College stated, "The entire educational structure of Yampa Valley College is centered around International Relations and the implementation of a broader and deeper understanding of world affairs."[16] Classes were taught all over downtown Steamboat Springs, from the Episcopal Church to the Harbor Hotel. The cafeteria was in Del's Jewelry building, and students lived in private homes or motels. There was a dorm in the large house on 9th and Oak streets, owned by Charles and Linda Ryan, who were also faculty members.[17]

Bogue was not only the recruiter; she was president, treasurer, and chief operating officer of Yampa Valley College. She dreamed of big money, but ran the college on a shoestring with help from the merchants and ranchers of Routt County.[18] By 1964 YVC had acquired at least eight houses in Steamboat Springs that were used as dorms and classrooms. The legal control of the college was the board of directors, thirty-five men and women handpicked by Bogue. The dominant members were merchants in Steamboat Springs, originally from rural areas, survivors of the Great Depression and World War II, politically and economically conservative.[19]

Among the small group of directors who took a real interest in the college, one man stood out as the dominant force: John Fetcher. Born in 1912 into a wealthy family in Winnetka, Illinois, a suburb of Chicago, he traveled to France with his family and learned to ski in Switzerland as a youth. He attended Harvard University, graduated with a bachelor's of science degree and stayed for a master's degree in engineering. In 1936 he took a job with the Budd Company in Philadelphia, where he worked until 1949. He and his brother quit their jobs in the East in 1949 and bought a ranch on the upper Elk River outside Steamboat Springs.[20]

Fetcher was one of a long line of easterners who came out West and tried to "out-cowboy the cowboys," mimicking the speech, dress, and what they perceived as the behavior of ranch culture. They came as romantics, but they found a culture of tough men, only sometimes tempered by compassion. Fetcher, although he aped cowboy culture, never quite understood the complexities of the lifestyle that he adopted. Some say he was often impatient to get his way.[21]

But he was also a unique combination of a concretely grounded individual and a visionary, and more importantly, a man of restless, Faustian energy.

In 1962 Fetcher's brother left the ranch partnership because, at least in Fetcher's own description, " . . . we were gradually going down the drain financially, and there just wasn't enough income for two families."[22] The Fetchers realized, as many had before and after them, that no matter how much money one invested in Routt County agriculture, the returns were minimal when compared to the work involved.

Fetcher, an expert skier and judge of ski jumping, decided to get into the ski business " . . . because I felt that I could do better with people than

31

John Fetcher in the 1970s.
Photo courtesy of *Steamboat Today* Photo
Archives. Digitized by Ken Proper.

with cows."[23] He had the vision to imagine that the social and economic changes taking place in America in the late 1950s and early 1960s could open up lucrative winter tourism for Steamboat Springs. He, along with Jim Temple and Marv Crawford, began to transform Storm Peak, immediately south of Steamboat Springs, into a downhill ski area.

The political culture of Colorado's Western Slope was in the early 1960s controlled by a coterie of politicians led by the conservative Democrat Congressman Wayne Aspinall and in Steamboat Springs by a small group of Republican businessmen and ranchers—including Fetcher—who cooperated with Aspinall. This group used their influence in Washington, D.C., to bring federal government money to the Western Slope. When the older mines—dug laterally into the hills to find narrow layers of coal—played out, new coal-mining technology opened up large seams to strip mining and the new power plants at Hayden and Craig, west of Steamboat Springs, welcomed the coal. The federal government subsidized both these new power plants and also the dams and reservoirs that provided needed water to cool the plants. In 1965 the Colorado Ute Power Plant in Hayden began operation. Construction began in 1966 on the dam for the new Steamboat Lake and work was completed on Stillwater Dam in south Routt County. The new airport outside of Hayden was dedicated in October 1966. Colorado Highway 131 was paved south to Wolcott where the new Interstate Highway 70 would open the Western Slope to skiers from the Front Range of Colorado.

John Fetcher was a large presence in all these developments. His behavior was based on three principles. The first was the financing of projects should use, if possible, tax dollars, preferably from the federal government. The second was, if federal dollars were not sufficient, then projects would have to be financed by the sale of land.[24] Fetcher's third principle, in business as in life, was always to have an exit strategy, which usually meant selling out to someone from outside the county who could bring in fresh money.[25]

The Yampa Valley College board of directors, led by John Fetcher, recognized that Lucy Bogue's ideal college was not economically sustainable. The Perry-Mansfield School of Theater and Dance was losing money, and in 1963 Charlotte Perry and Portia Mansfield, both getting older, decided to sell their school to Stephens College in Missouri.[26] Lowell Whiteman School was in financial trouble, and John Fetcher, also a director on the board of that school, proposed—although unsuccessfully—that the school and land be sold for a tourist attraction.[27]

Although Lucy Bogue had optimistically predicted that money would flow into the Yampa Valley College coffers, the college continued to operate on a slim budget. Tuition for the college was in fact quite high, $990 a year for two semesters, including room and board. This would have been about the same amount that a student would pay to go to Stanford University in 1962. And, the foreign students who received scholarships brought in no money.

Regretfully, it is difficult to obtain accurate figures for the early years of Yampa Valley College because the college did not follow standard bookkeeping practices. Donations from the town to the college diminished to $13,000 in 1963.[28] The college as yet had no campus and could hardly pay its teachers. John Fetcher's second principle had to come into play—it would be necessary to obtain land for a campus and sell some of it in order to build a campus and get financial stability— exactly what he was doing at the same time to build the ski area.[29]

On August 30, 1962, Bogue and other directors of Yampa Valley College came before the trustees of the Steamboat Springs town board and requested a donation of twenty acres of town land called the Bath House property, an empty tract of land between the hot springs pool and land that had been given for a new high school. A college campus there would have created a line of educational institutions in close proximity to one another extending to Strawberry Park. Lucy Bogue's husband, Art Bogue, was one of the town trustees, so there was a friendly atmosphere at the meeting. When the town attorney said that the town could not legally give the land to a private entity, the trustees voted for a five-year option to be given to the college to purchase the land at $10 an acre. The trustees then stipulated that if the land was not put to educational use after five years or if education did not take place there for two consecutive years, the land would revert back to the town.[30] This policy of "reversion" would become an important issue in the history of the college.

However, the twenty-acre Bath House property was not large enough to both support a college and a real-estate development. Without sufficient land, in the summer of 1963, the directors told Bogue that they had decided to close the college.[31] But there was one more option. On November 8, 1963, Harold Grear, the newly appointed budget director and dean of Yampa Valley College, appeared before the town trustees and asked that the previous option for the Bath House property be made certain. But he added a new request: that the town also sell Yampa Valley College thirty-five acres of town land for $10 an acre on Woodchuck Hill, located at the opposite end of town.[32]

The name "Woodchuck Hill" was due to its association with the Woodchuck irrigation ditch that originated at Soda Creek, a stream that flowed from the mountains above Strawberry Park into Steamboat Springs and then into the Yampa River. At the western edge of Steamboat Springs, the Yampa runs through a gap of Dakota sandstone.[33] Routt County's early settlers, in order to irrigate their land, dug ditches by hand and with mules or horses to carry water from the mountains, and in the late 1880s Routt County pioneer John H. Burroughs filed a water appropriation for this ditch. He originally envisaged that the Woodchuck

Woodchuck Hill in 1913 showing the narrow gap of the Yampa River. From Denver one enters the town heading north but soon the Yampa River and the highway turn toward the west, and at that point on the curve, Woodchuck Hill looms over the town. Any buildings on that hill would have prominence in Steamboat Springs. Photo by Outwest Photography. Courtesy of Tread of Pioneers Museum, Steamboat Springs, Colorado.

Ditch would end at Copper Ridge Gap, thus the name Woodchuck Hill. However, when the ditch was finally completed in 1909, it reached the cemetery property on the other side of Copper Ridge and never got as far as Woodchuck Hill.[34]

Woodchuck Hill is a steep, south-facing hill—its elevation starts at 6,688 feet and ends at 7,156 feet. Its flora consists of sagebrush, mountain mahogany, serviceberry and antelope shrubs, pinion-juniper woodland, scattered oak shrubs, and a variety of grasses. In an average year, 130 inches of snow falls on the hill that contains numerous small and large hot springs.[35] It is unsuited for agriculture.

When Yampa Valley College Dean and Budget Director Harold Grear first proposed Woodchuck Hill as a site for the college, the town trustees thought that the school district might be interested in some of the land and refused to give the college an option on it.[36] The next week there was a special meeting of the college directors and the town board.

35

The directors stated that the college wished to use both the Bath House and Woodchuck Hill properties as collateral to obtain a loan to build dormitories and classrooms. By this time Art Bogue was no longer a town trustee and the mood was different. The town board refused to validate the deal made for the Bath House property and refused the request for the Woodchuck Hill land because $10 an acre was much less than the actual value of the land and the thirty-five acres of Woodchuck Hill was the only remaining possible subdivision left in the town.[37]

Lucy Bogue was now in a desperate situation since without land Yampa Valley College would disappear. Then architect Victor Hornbein entered the picture. In the summer of 1963 Bogue took Hornbein and his partner, Ed White, to Woodchuck Hill and she described the experience in her book, *Miracle on a Mountain*:

> Vic Hornbein and Ed White were immediately infected by my dream . . . I took them to the top of Woodchuck Hill, where we could look out over the world stretched below, with the Yampa River shining silver in its green, green valley, and the distant hills stretching out blue and misty till they met the sky. 'Here,' I told them, 'you will build the World Center, a great building to which people from all over the earth will come for conferences to discuss peace, and culture, and interaction between nations.' I couldn't have said that to everyone, but Hornbein and White understood, and they thrilled to my wild dream.[38]

She wanted buildings on Woodchuck Hill that resembled Swiss chalets. "My vision of the campus had long been a group of alpine-style buildings in wood, stone, and white plaster, buildings of the earth and mountains, that would look as though they had been there for two hundred years," Bogue wrote.[39] Her drawings were featured in the first brochures of YVC.

By the end of 1963 Bogue was exhausted and sick, and Victor Hornbein was her last hope to save her college. She promised to nominate Craig Davidson as a figurehead president of the college while

Yampa Valley College brochure dated 1964 and signed by Lucy Bogue illustrating her concept for the buildings. Archives, Steamboat Springs Campus, Copyright Colorado Mountain College. Digitized by Ken Proper.

giving Hornbein complete control over not only the architecture of the new buildings but also over academics, public relations, and fundraising.

For the historian, several problems arise here. First, why would a successful architect from Denver take on the responsibility of running a college that involved a difficult drive of more than four hours. We do not know enough of Hornbein's personality to understand why he took on this task. Second, it is not clear if Lucy Bogue communicated the decision to elevate Hornbein to the directors of the college or to the faculty, and if not, general astonishment must have arisen when the news came out. We do know that Hornbein took his new tasks seriously and produced educational and architectural documents unique in the history of education in Colorado.[40]

In December 1963 Victor Hornbein visited with and lobbied the Steamboat Springs board of trustees. He sent the town a document entitled "Operational Concepts, Yampa Valley College" in early January 1964. Hornbein made it clear that he shared Bogue's educational vision, and he outlined the basis of a liberal arts college that expanded the educational philosophy of Yampa Valley College to include "a fully integrated course of study not limited to the humanities." He proposed teaching history and literature along a "central theme," not unlike what is done today at Colorado College in Colorado Springs. He explained how the college would be financed with capital, operating, and endowment funds; how educational development and the selection of faculty would be made; and he detailed building construction plans. Hornbein wrote to the mayor of Steamboat Springs on January 7, 1964, that he foresaw the college becoming " . . . the major industry in the city, bringing in large sums of money."[41]

On January 10, 1964, Bogue went before the town trustees and again asked for the conveyance of both the Bath House and the Woodchuck Hill properties. Hornbein's lobbying had done its job. The trustees now changed their stance, and on February 14 the town signed a contract with the Yampa Valley College for the sale of 34.65 acres on Woodchuck Hill.[42] The town's contract with YVC contained the same reversion clauses that the town had put on the Bath House property in 1962, including the stipulation that the deed would not be tendered until college buildings had actually been constructed and education begun.[43]

Later in 1964 the forty-acre parcel north of the town's land on Woodchuck Hill that had remained in private hands was bought by the college.[44] The land had been owned by John and Martha Marsell, but this very steep northern parcel was landlocked and of little value. In January 1964 Bogue wrote to Hornbein that the college was to buy this land, and she reported in a 1964 Yampa Valley College newsletter that the northwest forty acres was bought ". . . with gifts from Harold Grear, dean of the college, and from Craig Davidson, president-elect."[45]

Hornbein's architectural vision for the college was as imaginative as his educational ideals. Given the configuration of Woodchuck Hill, a campus could take two different forms: buildings could stay in the middle of the hill, on the most level ground, with a small semi-circular campus around one central axis; or buildings could use the middle and lower parts of the hill for an upper/lower campus plan.[46] Hornbein chose an upper/lower campus plan, with the first phase to be a dining room/ theater and dormitories on a lower level with classrooms in a separate building, all with a view of the town and mountains with terraces between the buildings and a covered walk connecting them. The style was to be a modified modernist version of Lucy Bogue's alpine architecture. The most striking feature was a two-story, semi-circular glass window that enclosed a stage to convert the dining hall into an auditorium that would look over the Yampa Valley and be a visible symbol of the college. Later

Drawing by Victor Hornbein. Courtesy of Western History Collection, Denver Public Library.

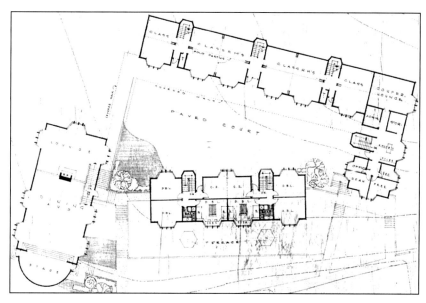

Architectural drawing by Victor Hornbein. Courtesy of Western History Collection, Denver Public Library.

phases would add additional buildings. The campus was to have two entrances: one from U.S. Highway 40 and one from Crawford Avenue.

Hornbein's use of the whole hill in his three-phase building plan was the most imaginative and creative campus design that was ever conceived for Woodchuck Hill. He estimated the cost of phase one to be $900,000 (equal to about $6.5 million in 2011 money). Hornbein, evidently swayed by Lucy Bogue's optimism and probably ignorant of the real wealth of Steamboat Springs, thought that he could raise the money locally. On March 20, 1964, he convinced the directors to sell twenty-year debentures, valued at $1,000, giving five percent interest, and secured by "real property."[47]

Debenture, Yampa Valley College. Archives, Steamboat Springs Campus, Copyright Colorado Mountain College. Digitized by Ken Proper.

Both Steamboat Springs and Yampa Valley College experienced a very busy year in 1964. George and Marian Tolles, former teachers at the Lowell Whiteman School, returned to Steamboat Springs to work for the college, and George opened a rathskeller in a basement room of the Cantina Restaurant as a meeting place for students and young people. The drinking age for beer in Colorado at that time was eighteen years.

In addition, Storm Peak was officially renamed "Mount Werner," a change reflecting the political clout of the Western Slope politicians.[48] It usually takes years or decades to change the name of a geological site in the United States.

John Fetcher received a $420,000 Small Business Administration loan from the federal government for the new ski area, and the new airport in Hayden got a large grant from the Federal Aviation Administration.

At the same time Hornbein and Ev Bristol worked tirelessly to raise money for the college. They thought they could sell at least 150 debentures in Steamboat Springs, but sold only ninety. They were hoping for federal governmental assistance because in December 1963 the U.S. Congress passed a "Facilities Rider" that assisted in the financing of college buildings as part of the "Higher Education Act."[49] However, the political combination of conservative Democrats and Republicans in northwest Colorado, very successful in their attempts to get federal money to finance dams, an airport, and a ski area, were not willing to lobby for the college; Hornbein got no support from the local politicians. The directors of the college tried to keep the drums beating, but the businessmen of the community were now looking to the new ski area as their economic savior.[50] The educational ideals of Strawberry Park were no longer as compelling.

At the end of 1964 Bogue had thought she would hand the reigns of the college over to Craig Davidson and Victor Hornbein. She was still president in January 1965 when the directors informed her that she was fired along with Davidson and Grear. In her book, *Miracle on a Mountain*, Bogue recorded her shock and surprise over this action.[51] She had been a tireless advocate of the Strawberry Park vision of liberal arts education and a successful recruiter of students, but she lacked an advanced academic degree, was a poor administrator, and did not understand finances.

Victor Hornbein wrote to Bogue expressing his sorrow over the failure of the fund drive, her illness, and the end of her career in higher education in Steamboat Springs.[52] She left Steamboat Springs and taught in Japan, went to the University of California at Berkeley to get a master's degree in literature, and taught at Mills College in Oakland, California. Hornbein continued to be an influential architect in Denver until his death in 1995.

Thus ended the first attempt to establish a college on Woodchuck Hill. The directors pulled the plug, and Steamboat Springs lost what would have been an imaginative liberal arts campus on Woodchuck Hill.

Lincoln Jones

IN 1965 AND 1966 ARCHITECT Lincoln Jones designed college buildings for Yampa Valley College that were unusual in their own right and surprising for a mountain town like Steamboat Springs. Years later I taught in those buildings and they became deeply entwined with my teaching career.

Lincoln "Linc" Jones was born in Chicago in 1925, spent his early childhood in Georgia and Wisconsin, and his high-school years back in Chicago.[1] During World War II he served in the U.S. Army Air Corps in Guam on bombers whose target was Japan. On the way to Guam, his unit stopped in Colorado—a life-changing moment for Jones, who immediately fell in love with the mountains. He had always wanted to be an architect, but at that time there was no architectural school in Colorado. So on his release from the army, he entered the University of Illinois, graduated from the School of Architecture in 1953, and immediately moved to Boulder.

At the University of Illinois, Jones was influenced by the organic modernism of Frank Lloyd Wright. In the 1950s he visited both Taliesin East and Taliesin West, Wright's educational studios. He also visited and was influenced by Bruce Goff, an architect at the University of Oklahoma who "was taking Wright's ideas to a new level."[2] In Boulder, Jones found the ideal town for his ideas. Home to the University of Colorado, with a population of 50,000 in the 1950s, it was the intellectual and cultural center of Colorado.

Boulder was the gathering place for architects influenced by the mid-century organic architecture of Frank Lloyd Wright, called "Usonian." In 1938 Wright originally used the term to characterize low-cost housing that he associated with the ideal of the "common people," but the term later became associated with all of Wright's "organic" modern architecture that was inspired by the American landscape. Here is where historical vocabulary gets tricky.

In architecture there was a second kind of modernism that originated in Europe called the International style. With roots in the German Bauhaus movement and led by Le Corbusier, Walter Gropius, and Mies van de Rohe, the International style favored structures that eschewed superfluous ornamentation, had flat roofs, and used reinforced concrete. While Wright used many of these same techniques, the two types of modernism in architecture were distinct and hostile to each other. Wright thought that nature still had ontological authority as a sender of messages, and many of his buildings fit into their natural environment, hugged the earth, and used materials to suggest warmth and comfort.[3]

In Europe nature had lost this ontological authority, and many of the International style buildings appeared to critics as harsh and heartless concrete slabs. Yet, to make matters even more complicated, both styles of modernism in architecture were actually a romantic rebellion against the manic valueless behavior of the marketplace and an attempt to use architecture to support a flourishing way of life.[4]

Chief among the Wright-inspired architects of Boulder was Charles A. Haertling, who designed buildings that were said to push "Usonian architecture to its expressionist margins."[5] What this meant was modern architecture, like art and literature, became by the mid-twentieth century a bit strange, uncanny, and difficult to understand. The World Affairs Conferences at the University of Colorado brought in uncanny and visionary architects such as Buckminster Fuller, whose presence would have been hard for a young, ambitious architect to ignore.[6] Lincoln Jones thrived in that atmosphere; he was moving toward his own brand of

Lincoln Jones in 1983.
Courtesy of *Steamboat Today* Photo
Archives. Digitized by Ken Proper.

eclectic architecture that combined Wright's organic approach and the International style with other influences.[7]

In 1953 Jones obtained an entry-level architectural position with the Boulder firm of Selby Wheeler and Carol B. Lewis. Wheeler & Lewis specialized in designing educational facilities, primarily elementary and secondary schools that were " . . . to provide an ideal environment for learning."[8] These schools were usually one-story, brick structures with large windows and strong horizontal lines that provided a modernist alternative to the traditional square, brick two-story buildings that had characterized Colorado schools before World War II. In addition, Wheeler & Lewis also designed churches. Both school and church architecture would give Lincoln Jones an entry into his profession, and this first apprenticeship would serve him well in future years.

In 1959 Jones left Wheeler & Lewis and formed a partnership with Tom Nixon (1928-1997), a Boulder native who earned a degree in architecture from Texas A & M in 1952 and was also a student of Bruce Goff in Oklahoma.[9] The architectural firm of Nixon & Jones designed many buildings in Boulder—residences, a school, churches,

First Christian Church of Boulder, Colorado, by architects Lincoln Jones and Tom Nixon. Courtesy of City of Boulder Planning Department.

a fire station, a medical clinic, and apartments. The firm also worked throughout Colorado: Faith Lutheran Church in Golden, Fremont County Courthouse, and high schools in Limon, Holly, and Granby. In 1962 they designed a courthouse for the town of Craig, just west of Steamboat Springs. Their most famous structure was the First Christian Church on 28th Street in Boulder, a building that reflected strong Frank Lloyd Wright influences with a cantilevered roof reminiscent of Wright's Unitarian Meeting House of 1947 and the Henry Neils house of 1949.[10] The First Christian Church was later called " . . . an iconic example of Boulder's original modernist architecture."[11]

In the middle 1960s the partnership of Nixon & Jones slowly and amicably dissolved. The men continued to be good friends and shared their love of automobile racing, both as spectators and as participants. Jones opened his own office on Pearl Street in Boulder. He was now married with four children, and that undoubtedly put more economic pressure on his professional life. He was in the uncomfortable position of lecturing on the theme of architectural creativity at the University of Colorado School of Architecture, while in his professional life he was still looking for an opportunity to showcase his creative talents. In the early 1960s a utopian architectural movement mirrored the ferment of the early John F. Kennedy presidential years, and Jones, with his close ties to the University of Colorado, may have been aware of the trend.[12]

By 1964 Jones realized that there was too much competition for architectural work on the Front Range of Colorado and that the Western Slope was the new frontier for economic development. He was attracted to Steamboat Springs where John Fetcher's new ski area had raised economic expectations. His first job was with the architect William Sayre on a master plan for the newly named Mount Werner Ski Area. Jones imagined a series of hexagonal buildings with overlapping roofs that were to be a series of shops and restaurants. This Wright-inspired design was used later in Jones' educational plans. Like many master plans, his drawings were used to encourage investors, but never actually made into reality.

In 1965 Jones moved with his family to Steamboat Springs and opened an architectural office. Jones was a workaholic and his output was prodigious. With the ever-present pipe in his mouth, Jones was a rapid executor of plans for additions, houses, schools, and churches.[13] He once expressed his love for Steamboat Springs to his colleague Bob McHugh:

> We live in a laid back Western town, with many natural unique features. It's mellow with very few pressures you find in most cities. There is not the pretentiousness which you find in Aspen or Vail. Character rather than money is where our values are found.[14]

Jones saw himself as a "professional volunteer" for non-profit organizations, including "my own practice." In Steamboat Springs he was active with St. Paul's Church, Arts Council, Audubon Society, Winter Sports Club, and Kiwanis service organization. He was something of a bon

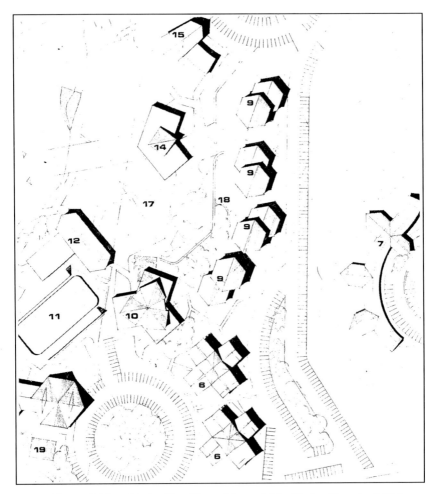

"Mount Werner Ski Area Master Plan, Phase 1," as published in the *Steamboat Pilot*, October 5, 1964. Digitized by Ken Proper.

vivant, accomplished artist, brilliant conversationalist, and his own best publicist.

Jones received his first real commission in Steamboat Springs from Western Management and Development for a condominium building at the base of the ski area. Jones here showed his penchant for striking vertical rooflines and strong horizontal lines. The building also demonstrated his concern for detail in the ornamentation of the pillars, and although modified, it is still standing today.

48

"Ski Area Condominiums." Drawing by Lincoln Jones. From the archives of Robert S. Ralston. Digitized by Ken Proper.

In a 1983 interview with former *Steamboat Pilot* writer Dee Richards, Jones claimed that he was the first modern architect in northwest Colorado, a pioneer.[15] This was not true. He was preceded in Steamboat Springs by Denver architect Eugene Sternberg, who designed the Yampa Valley Electric Association building in 1956, Hillcrest Apartments, Stukey house in 1960, and Chamber of Commerce building in 1961.[16] In 1965, just after Jones completed his first work in Steamboat Springs, Denver architect Tor Westgaard designed a modernist memorial for the late Buddy Werner that was later turned into a library.[17]

This is not to say that Steamboat Springs embraced creative architecture in the early 1960s. The town was an architectural blank slate on which anything could be drawn. In the late 1950s and early 1960s there was a tolerant atmosphere in the western United States that extended to people, behavior, and projects. For building, Steamboat Springs did not require a planning process or a building permit until after the early 1970s. Frankie Stetson, a rancher and politician who was a young man at the time, later recalled that "nobody gave a damn what anyone else did."[18]

Jones had a big ego. It was a time when creative people believed that they could transform their unique visions into a new reality. The famous architects of America were beginning to be called "starchitects," and

Robert Pietrowski. From *Yampa Valley College Yearbook,* 1966-1967. Archives, Steamboat Springs Campus, Copyright Colorado Mountain College. Digitized by Ken Proper.

Lincoln Jones thought of himself as the local version. He soon became well known in Steamboat Springs and made the acquaintance of a fellow Air Force veteran, Robert Pietrowski. After the firing of Lucy Bogue, Pietrowski had been hired by John Fetcher to be the president of Yampa Valley College.

Born in Cleveland in 1921, Pietrowski was tall—six foot five— handsome, always impeccably dressed, and polite. He held bachelor's and master's degrees from Stanford University and taught at Stanford, Utah State University, and Colorado A & M (now Colorado State University) in Fort Collins. He had international experience: in 1964 he had been in Brazil on a United States aid project undertaken by the University of California at Los Angeles. However, Pietrowski was not popular in Steamboat Springs. Both faculty and students were loyal to Lucy Bogue, and Bogue disliked Pietrowski at first sight, was jealous of his advanced degrees, and believed that he disliked women.[19] She did everything in her power to turn the community, faculty, and students against him. As a result, Pietrowski's wife was shunned by the Steamboat Springs community.[20]

After Bogue was terminated as president, she was given the role of vice president in charge of recruitment, for she was indeed a formidable recruiter of students. But "she never gave a second thought to the college" after she was fired and left for California, according to close friend George Tolles.[21] Pietrowski was then burdened with the additional task of recruiting students, which meant that he had to be away from the campus for long periods of time. The faculty saw him as a "money guy" and a "wheeler-dealer."[22] Because of the financial problems of the college, he took away scholarships for foreign students and angered the internationalist sympathies of the Strawberry Park teachers. He realized, as architect Victor Hornbein had before him, that for Yampa Valley College to compete for government money, it had to be accredited. To bolster the academic credentials of the college, he bought a two-story, log building on private land on Woodchuck Hill and moved Lucy Bogue's library for the college into it.[23]

Pietrowski and his family lived in Charlotte Perry's house in Steamboat Springs, and he communicated to all who would listen that he shared the same liberal arts vision of education as the Strawberry Park educators. His daughter remembers him saying, "Mrs. Bogue is the founder of the college and we are here to carry out her wishes and make this a great place for kids to go to school."[24] He believed in the liberal arts, high academic standards, and in really educating, not just giving students grades and a diploma.[25] He prevailed on the faculty to "review" the student body and eliminate those students who were not doing well academically.[26]

Yampa Valley College now owned Woodchuck Hill, but because of the reversion clause that the Steamboat Springs trustees inserted in the deed, the college could only keep the property if buildings were constructed and classes taught. Pietrowski inherited the campus architectural plans of Victor Hornbein and throughout the summer of 1965 worked with Hornbein on a campus for the college. But Hornbein's plans were expensive—$900,000—and called for a first phase residential hall of only fifty students.[27] Hornbein's own calculations for financial success were predicated on a student body of 500 students.[28] Something did not make sense, and by the autumn of 1965 Hornbein withdrew as architect for the college.[29] Lincoln Jones was then hired as architect for the college in November 1965.

Although there is no documentary evidence, one would have to assume that Pietrowski, coming from northern California, and Jones, having taught at the University of Colorado, were aware that the 1960s were an exciting time for American campus architecture. The University of California at Santa Cruz, begun in 1961 with a master plan by John Carl Warnecke, finally opened in 1965, and architects William Turnbull and Charles W. Moore were planning Kresge College, finally built in 1970 as a living-learning center with students and professors living and studying communally, as in Thomas Jefferson's academic village.[30] Also, in 1965 Edward Durrell Stone designed the buildings for Windham College, where Lucy Bogue had visited and was in some sense a model for Yampa Valley College.

Pietrowski's first problem was financial. In order to get money for construction, there would have to be a bond issue with Woodchuck Hill used as collateral. Yet the Steamboat Springs town trustees kept the land from being deeded to the college until buildings were constructed. The first step that Pietrowski made was to have the directors of Yampa Valley College form a public entity, the Yampa Valley College Building Authority—controlled by the same small group of directors that led YVC—with tax-exempt status and the ability to issue bonds.[31] These directors then went before the town trustees and asked them to modify the reversionary clause so that the Steamboat Springs school district would "accept as a gift those facilities so financed by the Building Authority" when the bonds were paid off in thirty years.[32] With this guarantee, the trustees voted on June 10, 1966, that even without buildings a deed should be conveyed to YVC "for a tract without restrictions" on Woodchuck Hill.[33] Bonds worth $900,000 were sold by Kirchner & Co. of Denver. However, unlike the earlier debenture sale of Victor Hornbein, the buyers of these bonds were not residents of Steamboat Springs, but were institutional and private investors throughout the West.[34]

Why did the bonds sell so well? In 1965 the Yampa Valley College owned sixty-five acres of Woodchuck Hill, but the authority only bought and leased back to the college a small tract of 1.45 acres in the middle of the hill, an area where the college buildings were to be built. The bondholders' collateral was to be the college buildings on the small tract. The John Fetcher scheme—sell land to finance projects—was in operation: the rest of the land could be sold by YVC for development to pay off the bondholders.[35] The Steamboat Springs school district would obtain ownership when the bonds were totally redeemed.[36]

That the bonds were restricted to the small tract meant that Lincoln Jones' architectural plans for a campus would be limited to 1.45 acres and not the entire Woodchuck Hill. He was thereby forced to design the first buildings of a projected campus on the middle of Woodchuck Hill.[37]

The directors of Yampa Valley College were no doubt aware of this disadvantage, but they were more concerned with the ability of the college to pay the interest on the bonds. John Fetcher's three principles were still in play here: hope for some federal funding if the college could get accredited, if that failed, then sell some property surrounding the small tract to private developers, and if that failed, sell the college.

Jones' first drawings for the Yampa Valley College campus, published in the *Steamboat Pilot* under the name of Nixon & Jones, were not visionary, but were reminiscent of the buildings that Jones had designed for Wheeler & Lewis—one-story, horizontal high-school buildings.

Surprising changes took place between March and April of 1966. Jones left Nixon & Jones and struck out on his own, and he produced a different and bold set of plans for the campus of Yampa Valley College.

Jones knew that Woodchuck Hill was a unique architectural site, and he spent hours walking it and getting views from all angles.[38] His plans, featuring hexagonal structures and a cantilevered roof, reflected his earlier work on the First Christian Church in Boulder and the

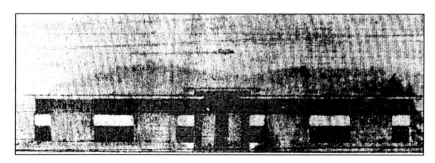

"Lincoln Jones' first plans for Yampa Valley College," as published in the *Steamboat Pilot*, March 24, 1966. Digitized by Ken Proper.

unused master plan for the ski hill in Steamboat Springs. Jones' buildings revealed their dependence on the ideas of Frank Lloyd Wright, but were also eclectic in their reliance on other architects. While there is no documentary evidence to show influences on Jones, his Yampa Valley College buildings show some resemblance to the 1960 buildings at Michigan State University designed by R. R. Calder.[39]

Jones wanted to get away from the dormitory as jail or hotel—long, horizontal buildings with inner hallways that had doors monotonously spaced. His design featured two hexagonal structures—the dormitory rooms—joined in the middle by a large, open classroom space.

The most prominent feature of the buildings was the cantilevered roofs that resembled the First Christian Church of Boulder. That school and church architecture might be related goes back to Jones' work with Wheeler & Lewis and ties to Thomas Jefferson's model of liberal education. One of Jones' predilections was for the half-mansard flat roof, considered in the 1960s a cheap and easy way to redesign a building, in this case made more modern by strong horizontal lines.

A mere physical description of the buildings does not convey their uniqueness. In our spoken language, we are comforted by hearing words that are familiar, and we are disturbed by strange syntax and vocabulary. In architecture, structures also speak to us as familiar, or unfamiliar. One of the themes of the avant-garde in literature, art, and architecture in the twentieth century was to shock by deliberately making something strange.[40] Lincoln Jones' college buildings were the *Finnegan's Wake* of architecture for Steamboat Springs.[41]

The cantilevered roofs of the college buildings immediately brought one's thoughts to a church, and on entering a church, one expects to see a dramatic entrance hallway or sanctuary. But here there was no large entrance hall, in fact no entrance at all, no place for one to get one's bearings. Instead one was placed immediately into a labyrinth of corridors and thirty-degree angles. When Freud in the nineteenth century was lost in a maze of city streets, he used the word "uncanny" to describe the feeling of something both intimate and foreign at the same time, the transformation of something homey into something very unhomey, in

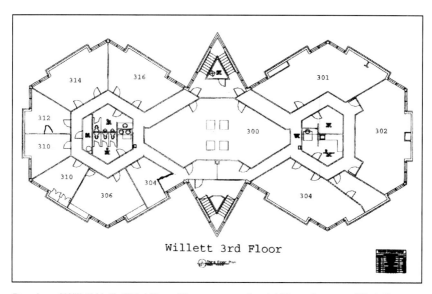

Drawing of Willett Hall's Third Floor. The rooms on the right have been modified; the original dorm rooms resembled those on the left. From Maintenance Department, Steamboat Springs Campus. Copyright Colorado Mountain College.

German *unheimlich*. I will here speak from experience: even after thirty years in these buildings, sometimes I would walk in and find myself lost.

Why did Jones design such structures? He has left us no documentary evidence, but it is apparent that he was not thinking about the sensibilities of Steamboat Springs, but of the students who would inhabit these buildings as both dormitories and classrooms. Young men and women going to college in the mid-1960s were usually leaving home for the first time and living in a completely new environment. Most college dormitories at this time were built like prisons, and the experience was often alienating, especially for women, who were locked in at night. Jones understood, as was indeed the case, that young people would soon feel at home in his *unheimlich* surroundings and, in fact, come to feel a strong attachment to their strangeness. The figure of the labyrinth had long been used in Europe, in both pre-Christian and Christian contexts, as a learning device, and here Jones deliberately designed the uncanny as educational structure.[42] The students who first lived in these structures grew to see them as home. They liked the idea of staggering out of their dorm rooms in the morning and walking a few feet to class.[43] Women lived on separate floors than men, and it was one of the first, if not the first, college building in America where women were not locked in at night.[44] The first students in the Lincoln Jones buildings were not just feeling uncanny—they were being uncanny.[45] From this uncanny nature came a negation of monotony and boredom and a positive architecture of enjoyment.[46]

The ground-breaking for the first building was on May 6, 1966, although the *Steamboat Pilot* reported that " . . . some details are yet to be worked out."[47] The college buildings were stick-frame with plywood walls covered with red brick; they had modernist flat roofs. Jones thought that flat roofs would collect snow that would act as insulation in the winter.[48] The budget was limited; each building was 22,000 square feet and the cost was $17 a square foot. Construction was as inexpensive as possible because the three buildings would consume all of the money from the sale of the bonds.[49]

The first building was named after Ray Monson, a district attorney in Steamboat Springs, who had been instrumental in urging the town to donate land for civic improvements and who died in January 1966.[50] In the spring of 1967 Willett Hall, named after a famous doctor in Steamboat Springs, was completed, although the cantilevered roof collapsed during construction and a post had to be installed to hold it up. Bogue Hall, named after Lucy Bogue, was completed in the fall of 1967.[51]

At the end of September 1966 Lincoln Jones and Robert Pietrowski and their wives were feted at a banquet given by the directors of Yampa Valley College. Pietrowski gave a moving speech that emphasized the continuing physical growth—more buildings—on Woodchuck Hill.[52]

On the surface, everything was going well—Pietrowski was a confident man who thought that if he built a college, students would come. Pietrowski was friendly with the rancher Ferrington "Ferry" Carpenter—who had nothing to do with the college after an initial personal contribution of $10,000—but who may be seen as offering an alternative scenario to that of John Fetcher. Rather than sell land surrounding the buildings to pay the bonds, a larger campus would attract more students

Lucy Bogue Hall. Photo by Ken Proper.

and the resulting financial success would allow the college to meet its bond obligations. Jones and Pietrowski were motivated by the "build it and they will come mentality." They continued to envision a bigger campus with a large library and administration-classroom building next

Willett Hall showing the post holding up the cantilevered roof. Photo by Ken Proper.

to the three living-learning centers.[53] On November 23, 1966, Pietrowski addressed the Steamboat Springs Chamber of Commerce about future plans for an expanded campus and showed illustrations by Lincoln Jones to explain how he envisioned the full campus.[54]

Photograph of the model of the projected Yampa Valley College campus as prepared by Lincoln Jones. Actual model is held by the Archives, Steamboat Springs Campus, Copyright Colorado Mountain College. Photograph by Sandy Kent. Permission granted by Glen Jones and Sandy Kent.

However, the students did not come, or not in the numbers that would have sustained the college. Lucy Bogue, who had been a superb recruiter, had left for California. This forced Pietrowski to travel widely to recruit, but he also had to supervise the day-to-day operations of the college and the new construction. Because tuition, room and board in 1966 cost $1,025, about the same as elite, private colleges, in the fall of 1966 only 143 students had enrolled.[55]

As 1964 merged into 1965 strange social noises were faintly heard in Colorado, coming from the East and West coasts like the rumble of thunder heard in the distant mountains. The Vietnam War was heating up and inner-city rage was growing. The children of the suburbs, reacting against conformity, were coming to college with different ideas than their predecessors. However, the merchants of Steamboat Springs were talking about the 1964-1965 ski season that was "the best in Colorado history."[56] They chose not to notice the warning clouds on the horizon.

By 1966 the turbulent youth culture that had earlier only been a faint noise became much louder in Steamboat Springs. Hippies appeared in town, there were protests against the Vietnam War, and the students at Yampa Valley College were no longer as well behaved nor as carefully dressed. Unlike Lucy Bogue, who recruited in the East, Pietrowski had a special relationship with Philip Curtis, director of admissions at Menlo College in Northern California.[57] More and more students came from the West Coast where the cultural changes of the 1960s were more pronounced. The students at YVC were not as unruly or radical as on other college campuses, but in conservative Steamboat Springs they were seen as a foreign invasion. A particular thorn seemed to be the student David Roach, whose well-written articles in the student newspaper harshly criticized both the college administration and the town.[58]

The mood of Steamboat Springs and the West had changed. Rural culture that in the 1950s accepted an easy tolerance of difference became intolerant and violent. Hippies were pulled off the streets in Laramie, Wyoming, and Fort Collins by cowboys and had their heads shaved. A mood of hysteria gripped the West.[59] Brian Allen, son of entertainer Steve Allen, and two other students got into a fight with cowboys in May 1966 that ended in court.[60] In September 1966, on the day the new Lincoln Jones dormitory opened, four students got drunk at the Cave Inn, south of Steamboat Springs, and ran off the road at the sharp corner by the hot springs pool on Lincoln Avenue. Three were killed, further convincing townspeople that the college was out of control.[61] Gerald Rudolph, history professor at Yampa Valley College, wrote, "It seemed almost from the moment we moved up on the hill, student-townspeople relations became strained . . . and these relations worsened as more of the students began growing their hair long and smoking pot."[62] Pietrowski and the faculty tried to deal with the students in "an informed, firm but fair consistent judicious way."[63] The students did not help matters by wearing long hair, driving fast through town, partying, and fighting cowboys in bars. The conservative, rural-raised directors of YVC were angry, scared, and not inclined to be judicious toward students. They urged "harsh and draconian" punishments,[64] initiated police searches of the dormitories, and began to rethink the whole idea of a college.

Disgruntled students hanged an effigy of President Robert Pietrowski. From the *Yampa Valley College Yearbook*, 1966-1967. Archives, Steamboat Springs Campus, Copyright Colorado Mountain College. Digitized by Ken Proper.

When the students came back from Thanksgiving vacation in late November 1966 they found the cafeteria closed, and they hanged Pietrowski in effigy from the newly built dormitory. It was the last straw. In early December Pietrowski and the faculty of Yampa Valley College invited the business community to a meeting. It was supposed to be a joyful celebration of the college. The college served lithium water from a famous Steamboat Springs location, but the businessmen refused to drink it. George Sauer, a director of YVC and superintendent of schools, got the biggest applause when he bragged that the Steamboat Springs high-school football team could now beat Craig. The meeting was both tragedy and farce.[65]

The idea that college enrollment growth would sustain the college was not exaggerated, it was just a bit before its time. By the mid-1970s, when the Steamboat Ski Area began to achieve status and recognition, it would have been possible to recruit 500 or more students for a quality liberal arts college. But in 1966 the conservative directors of the college saw only difficult bond obligations, rowdy students, and a college president who wanted to expand the college beyond the small tract and imperil the ability to privately develop Woodchuck Hill. The directors had moved to the position of John Fetcher: it was time to sell the college to someone else.[66]

A week later during the board of director's November meeting, the directors voted to end Robert Pietrowski's contract and began to look for an exit strategy. The dream of Lucy Bogue for an independent liberal arts college in Steamboat Springs came to an end.

Robert Pietrowski went on to have a distinguished career with the California Educational Association. Lincoln Jones stayed in Steamboat until 1983 and continued to design imaginative buildings. His college buildings remained on Woodchuck Hill, on the horizon of Steamboat Springs.

Colorado Mountain College

IN THE SPRING OF 1967 the directors of Yampa Valley College ended the contract of President Robert Pietrowski because, under the pressure of student disruption and impending financial crises, they had forsaken the ideal of a liberal arts college and moved to John Fetcher's third principle—an exit strategy. They hired a series of men to bring some order to the college and make it marketable.[1]

At some point in 1967 the name of the college was changed to Colorado Alpine College because it was thought that by moving up the college in alphabetical order it would help recruit students and that the name "Colorado" would mean more to prospective students than "Yampa Valley."[2] On Woodchuck Hill, the log house that Pietrowski bought for the college was now made into an administration building, and the library was moved to Bogue Hall.

For the students and faculty, life went on. In an article for *Rocky Mountain Rural Life,* the publication of the Yampa Valley Electric Association, the president of the college, Richard Roper, emphasized the liberal arts commitment, with students getting bachelor's of arts degrees in humanities, social sciences, international studies, administrative studies, and creative arts. "Process is more important than product. People are more important than books. Controversy in the marketplace of ideas is more important than acquiescence and assent. Students are more important than courses," Roper added.[3]

On a recruiting tour in New Jersey in 1967, a representative of the college who was addressing potential students said, "The basic Liberal Arts curriculum is designed to serve those who desire a general education as the foundation for continuing personal growth and study."[4] But underneath this continuity of education, the college was on life support. It was neither able to sustain itself financially nor to put money away to pay the bond issue that financed the buildings.

In November 1968 John Fetcher had lunch on the West Coast with a group of fellow Republicans. Richard Nixon had just been elected president of the United States, and the West Coast Republicans were jubilant. One of Nixon's "Republican Associates"—an informal California group that raised money for him—was William C. Rust, a Methodist minister born in 1918. Rust was president of California Western University, at that time loosely affiliated with the Methodist Church. Fetcher could not believe his good luck: he had found the man to buy Colorado Alpine College.

William Rust was some combination of educational visionary and fast-talking salesman. Seen in a positive light, he had a dream of an international academic empire that would " . . . bring together people of the world based on the belief that neither nations nor individuals can flourish in isolation."[5] From another perspective, he used his Republican connections to get free title to government land—usually obsolete military bases—because he said that he was going to use the land for educational purposes. He would then build a small campus and mortgage the rest of the land to raise money. He changed the name of California Western University to United States International University (USIU) and expanded its acreage from 200 to 2,400 acres.[6] He severed ties with the Methodist Church, appointed a board for this new university that consisted of his Republican friends from San Diego, and in 1969 assumed the power to sell stocks, bonds, and securities for the university. The main campus in San Diego moved from its original site to a former military base, and he established auxiliary campuses in London, Nairobi, and Mexico City.

Rust and Fetcher shared the same economic principles: in order to make projects successful, rely on government funds for land and use the land as mortgage collateral to get cash. They also shared the same idealistic vision of a college liberal arts education that would emphasize international studies. It would be reasonable to assume that Fetcher and the directors of Colorado Alpine College believed that Rust would continue the liberal arts tradition on Woodchuck Hill, although no documentary evidence has as yet been found to support this idea. The directors of Colorado Alpine College conveyed the assets of the school to United States International University. From Rust's viewpoint, it was a sweet deal. He did not have to pay anything for the land in Steamboat Springs, and he simply had to agree to take over the lease on the buildings designed by Lincoln Jones—about two acres in the "small tract" that was owned by the Yampa Valley College Building Authority— and thus be responsible to pay off the bonded indebtedness. In return Rust's university received title to the remaining sixty-five acres of land on Woodchuck Hill that he could then mortgage or sell.[7]

Just after graduation in the spring of 1969, the students of Colorado Alpine College found out that their school had been sold and that they had been given diplomas from an institution that no longer existed. They organized into SOS—"Save Our College"—marched down Lincoln Avenue and railed against the directors of the college, but to no avail. Rust came to Steamboat Springs and promised the grateful townsfolk that he had arrived "to clean up the pig pen on the hill."[8] Little did the good citizens know that at this time Rust was $5 million in debt and was being investigated by U.S. Senator Mark Hatfield for a land grab in Oregon.[9]

Rust was never very interested in using the Steamboat Springs campus of United States International University for education. It enrolled fewer than one hundred students a year, and the buildings were mostly unused. He sold the library, begun by Lucy Bogue, to a school in North Dakota, and he also disposed of much of the equipment in the buildings. He fired most of the faculty except for a skeleton crew. Under his benign neglect, strange happenings took place on Woodchuck Hill.

John Fetcher decided to build a rope tow for a ski run, but it never quite worked.[10] Owen Geer, campus director in 1971-1972, took a bulldozer to the hill and helped Fetcher carve out a ski run and then created a lake and a parking lot. In 1972-1973 Bill Doxey was campus director, and finally in 1974, with eighty students left, George Tolles became director of the campus.[11] At that point all financial aid from San Diego ended and the remaining teachers—Tolles, Fran Conlon, and Carol Samson—continued to teach without pay.

In 1971 Rust mortgaged the sixty-five acres he controlled on Woodchuck Hill to a group called USF Investors.[12] In 1974 these same investors sued United States International University: a levy was placed upon the property, and the sheriff locked the doors of the buildings.[13] When USIU declared bankruptcy, a Denver district court conveyed the land to Independence Mortgage Trust of San Diego.[14] In 1979 the mortgage was sold to "Steam Realty," a New York holding company of Citibank.

After United States International University took over in 1968, there was no upkeep of the Lincoln Jones buildings. Since the buildings were to revert back to the school district when the bonds were paid, there was no reason for Rust to put any money into them. After 1975 some portion of the buildings were used by Colorado Northwest Community College (CNCC) as an outreach center and by the Steamboat Springs school district for continuing education, but for the most part the buildings were empty or at times rooms were rented out to anyone who wanted a place to sleep in the town. By 1978 the buildings had dangerously deteriorated. Lincoln Jones later told Dee Richards of the *Steamboat Pilot*, "I guess that my greatest excitement and greatest depression has come with the college. It's been hurtful to see the buildings disintegrate."[15]

Nineteen seventy-nine was a crucial year for Woodchuck Hill. Steam Realty was about to foreclose on the sixty-five acres of the hill that did not contain the college buildings. The first payout of $265,000 on the 1966 bonds—with the collateral of two acres where the college buildings were located—was due in June. It looked as if both the remnants of the college and the land surrounding it would have to be sold. Citibank,

Bill Hill.
Courtesy of *Steamboat
Today* Photo Archives.
Digitized by Ken Proper.

the parent of Steam Realty, had been sending teams of men from New York to Steamboat Springs to market Woodchuck Hill. David Combs, whose family owned land adjacent to Woodchuck Hill, was negotiating with Steam Realty for a half-acre of land for a new subdivision and was contemplating the marketing of the whole hill.[16] Time was running out, but happily for the college if not for Steamboat Springs, the country was in an economic recession and real-estate values were depressed.

In 1979 the Yampa Valley Foundation, headed by a banker named Rex Peilstick, was founded with the idea of supporting a new college in Steamboat Springs. The real impetus behind the foundation was a man named Bill Hill. Hill was born in Hebron, Nebraska, in 1934, graduated with a degree in business administration from Nebraska Wesleyan University in 1956 and stayed there as director of alumni affairs. That first job cemented his future in higher education and nonprofits as a fundraiser and booster, and he moved frequently within that milieu.[17] He was a born public relations man, always smiling and remembering your name, always optimistic. In 1977 he came to Steamboat Springs as a tourist, saw an ad for a job as Chamber of Commerce director, applied, and was hired in 1978.

It must have seemed to Bill Hill that his whole peripatetic life had been a dress rehearsal for the campaign to reestablish a college in Steamboat Springs. In 1979 he quit his job with the Chamber and became director of the Yampa Valley Foundation. His first task was to negotiate with William Rust, who still held the lease on the small parcel of land on Woodchuck Hill where the college buildings stood. Both men were Methodists with the gift of speech of a John Wesley, and both had devoted their lives to getting money from others through the force of their personalities. Nevertheless, they had very different agendas.

Rust, his empire crumbling around him, wanted to hold on to some power and money, and Hill wanted to resurrect the college on Woodchuck Hill. The United States International University had just received a windfall of more than $300,000 because a tax lien was released by the Internal Revenue Service, and Rust told Hill that the university would honor the payment schedule on the bonds even after the Yampa Valley Foundation took over management of the small parcel. Rust actually placed $300,000 with the Central Bank of Denver for that purpose.[18]

In September 1979 Hill sent out a letter under the heading of "Bondholders Protection Committee" stating that United States International University would make payments under an amended lease, and he also wrote a prospectus for an independent "Colorado Alpine Campus" predicated on the belief that USIU and Rust would pay the principle and interest on the bonds and buy out the Steamboat Springs school district lease agreement.[19]

By 1980 it was clear that United States International University and Rust had no intention of honoring these promises or releasing any money from the Denver bank, and the pressure from Steam Realty to develop Woodchuck Hill intensified. Still hoping for an independent Steamboat Springs college, Hill turned to private donors and then to the government for money, this time to the state of Colorado. Colorado Senate Bill 87, proposed by local state legislators, was to grant the proposed college $120,000 in emergency funds and prepare the way for a bond issue vote in Routt County. It was killed in the Senate Education Committee by one vote.[20]

With his dream of an independent college in Steamboat Springs gone, Hill turned to other scenarios. The most obvious one would be to partner with the community college in Craig and form a college in the Yampa Valley with two centers.[21] But the Craig community college was already part of Colorado Northwest Community College centered in Meeker and Rangely, towns very distant from Steamboat Springs. The third alternative was to become part of Colorado Mountain College (CMC). The presidents of CNCC and CMC traveled to Steamboat Springs to debate and press their cases, and it appeared that most of the interested parties in Steamboat Springs were attracted to Colorado Mountain College.

With its administrative center in Glenwood Springs, and campuses in Leadville and the Roaring Fork Valley, Colorado Mountain College comprised a vast territory in Western Colorado, including the resort towns of Aspen and Vail. It was not part of the state system of community colleges but was supported by mill levies in its district. The story told is that when Bill Hill brought this proposal to the Colorado Commission on Higher Education, its members were skeptical until the intervention of John Fetcher. Then the "miracle" occurred and the college on Woodchuck Hill was "saved."[22] John Fetcher had done little to help Hill finance an independent college. But the Colorado Mountain College option satisfied his criteria—sell out to some outside entity that used tax-supported dollars.[23] F. Dean Lillie, the president of Colorado Mountain College, also had his financial demands: CMC would not take on the Steamboat Springs campus unless the entire college district, including Routt County, voted to include Steamboat Springs as a tax district with a certain mill levy. Lillie wanted Steamboat Springs because he was in the process of turning CMC from its emphasis on mining to an emphasis on ski resorts.

Bill Hill has described the fight for the mill levy vote in his chapter in Lucy Bogue's *Miracle on a Mountain*. The vote passed in the Steamboat Springs school district but not in south or west Routt County. Nevertheless, it was enough to satisfy Lillie.[24] In the negotiations with Steam Realty some land on Woodchuck Hill was sold to David Combs in return for a road easement through his subdivision. The log cabin administrative house owned by the college was sold to Harry Dike in December 1981.[25] In return, Colorado Mountain College paid off the bond obligations and bought the remaining land on Woodchuck Hill from Steam Realty.[26] The future of higher education on Woodchuck Hill would now be determined by Colorado Mountain College.

Harvard on the Yampa

LIKE MOST COMMUNITY COLLEGES in 1981 Colorado Mountain College was an institution whose administrators believed that higher education should be vocational and practical. Its two residential campuses—Leadville and the Roaring Fork Valley, called the East and West campuses, and outreach centers—Vail, Aspen, Eagle, Rifle, Buena Vista, Breckenridge—paid only slight attention to the ideal of liberal arts. The organizational problem for the college was that of centrifugal force since each campus and center had different personalities. The addition of Steamboat Springs, with its educated population and its long tradition of liberal arts education added to the complexity of the college. The district office in Glenwood Springs had the job of enforcing uniformity and deciding how much local autonomy to tolerate. The first conflict with Steamboat Springs came with the naming of the campus. The district office wanted to name it the "North Campus," but Bill Hill, director of Yampa Valley Foundation, insisted that there be some linkage with the history of Steamboat Springs and insisted on "Alpine Campus."[1]

Hill did not have any problem with the vocational bias of Colorado Mountain College because he was more interested in vocational education and business courses than in the liberal arts.[2] The Strawberry Park model of Lucy Bogue was less important to him than the business needs of Steamboat Springs, such as ski business and resort management.

71

But the Strawberry Park model of liberal arts reasserted itself despite this bias due to a strange twist of fate.

Colorado Mountain College President F. Dean Lillie was a forceful and authoritarian administrator, "aggressive and into hegemony."[3] After the Alpine Campus joined CMC, Lillie made all the college administrators resign and reapply for their jobs or other jobs in a college-wide reorganization. He gave George Bagwell, an administrator and former professor at the Leadville campus, the choice: become the academic dean in the district office or become the dean of the Alpine Campus. Bagwell chose Steamboat Springs.

George Bagwell was born in Littlefield, Texas, in 1949. His father was a mechanical engineer and his mother an office manager. When George was six-months old the family moved to the San Joaquin Valley of California. His family later moved to San Diego where his father worked in defense industries. Bagwell attended high school in San Diego and then went to San Diego State University and earned a bachelor's degree in social science and a master's degree in anthropology and psychology. He was a part-time instructor at San Diego Mesa Community College in 1974 when he saw an ad in the *Chronicle of Higher Education* for a job on the East Campus of the still young Colorado Mountain College, which opened in 1967. He got the job, taught social science, and in 1977 became the director of arts, sciences, and general studies. In 1982 he came to Steamboat Springs.

When F. Dean Lillie selected Bagwell for the Alpine Campus, Lillie said, "Your job is to bring them into the Colorado Mountain College fold."[4] But Bagwell did not bring Alpine Campus into the CMC "fold." He immediately identified with Steamboat Springs and its liberal arts historical tradition. He ended many of the vocational programs at the Alpine Campus, horseshoeing, diesel mechanics, electrical, and instead reemphasized liberal arts and the student's ability to transfer to four-year colleges.[5] Every residential campus of CMC had a "cadillac program"—ski area technology at Timberline and veterinary studies and photography at Spring Valley. Bagwell decided that the "cadillac program" at the Alpine Campus would be the liberal arts transfer program.

George Bagwell in the 1980s.
Courtesy of George Bagwell.
Digitized by Ken Proper.

Bagwell inherited a campus in physical shambles. He later wrote, "The three buildings originally designed and built to be dormitories, Willett, Bogue and Monson halls, were in disrepair. Floors were literally falling in, roofs were leaking, windows and doors were broken . . . the library had been completely dismantled."[6] Monson Hall was actually boarded up, and rooms were occupied by vagrants and transients. With financial aid from the district office, Bagwell was able to repair the buildings. Willett Hall was transformed into a cafeteria, classroom, and faculty offices; Monson into a library and dormitory rooms; and Bogue into a dormitory.

Not only did Bagwell have to fight to get money to repair the buildings, but he also had to contend with the strong administrative prejudice of the district office against another residential campus. The whole idea of "living-learning" centers in cheap, plywood structures had been tried at the East and West campuses in the 1970s and had been given up as unsuitable for community colleges.[7] By skillful infighting, Bagwell prevailed in making Alpine Campus residential and academic.[8]

Bagwell chose George Tolles to guide academic life at the Alpine Campus. Tolles was born in 1929 in Toledo, Ohio, and attended Ohio State University, graduating with a bachelor's degree in history and a teaching credential.[9] After college he joined the U.S. Coast Guard, went through officer training, and spent three years in Louisiana and Texas searching cargo ships coming from Iron Curtain countries. After the coast guard, he bummed around Europe, found out that the G.I. Bill would pay for foreign education, and went to school in Innsbruck, Germany, for two years.[10] He then spent five years in the U.S. Foreign Service, serving in Washington, D.C.; Rotterdam (Netherlands); and Cali (Colombia). His wife Marian had relatives in Craig and he first motored through Steamboat Springs in 1957. He remembers drinking water from the lithium springs on Twenty Mile Road. While he was attending the Thunderbird School of International Management in Arizona, he found a magazine in the school library with an advertisement for a teacher of Spanish and history at the Lowell Whiteman School in Steamboat Springs. Tolles applied and got the job, took a year's leave from the foreign service, and taught at Whiteman. He and Marian lived with Gertrude Fetcher, former sister-in-law of John Fetcher, and formed a lifelong friendship with her, as they did with Lucy Bogue, who was then teaching at the Whiteman School. Tolles went back to the foreign service after one year, but when Lucy Bogue started Yampa Valley College, he returned to Steamboat Springs to teach in 1964. Realizing that as a college teacher he would need an advanced degree, in 1967 he left Steamboat Springs to attend the University of Pittsburg where he received a master's degree in international relations.

When Tolles returned to Steamboat Springs in the fall of 1969, he found that his old college had disappeared and been replaced by the United States International University. Most of the faculty had been fired, but Tolles had sent many boxes of books back early to his office and he occupied it on his return, telling William Rust that "I come with the college." He taught on Woodchuck Hill until 1974, when USIU folded. From 1975 to 1980 he taught elementary and high-school classes in Steamboat Springs.

When George Bagwell came to Alpine Campus as dean in 1982, Olive Morton, who became the dean for community education, convinced him to hire Tolles as one of the first instructors at the college. Tolles taught political science and history there for fifteen years. His

George Tolles teaching in the 1990s. Courtesy of *Steamboat Today* Photo Archives. Digitized by Ken Proper.

specialty was a course called "Great Decisions" that brought in a healthy mix of townspeople and students for a discussion of contemporary world affairs. Tolles was one of the few scholars who predicted the fall of the Berlin Wall before it happened and was one of the first academics in America to understand the importance of Islam for the modern world. He was skeptical of educational administrators—he often said that their job was to take care of the buildings and make sure the blackboards were clean and "then leave us alone so that we can teach."[11]

At some point in the 1970s Tolles was watching a well driller dowse for water in the Tree Haus subdivision across from Steamboat Ski Hill and tried it himself. He discovered that he had another calling: he became known in Routt County as a man who could tell you where to drill for water. But he also dowsed for the proper place to locate structures according to earth energy lines.[12] John Vickery, assistant campus dean in charge of instruction, tells the following story about Tolles:

> When Monson Hall was finally getting fixed up in the early 1980s one dorm room caused problems; the walls were painted black, its occupants always in trouble. Tolles said it was because the room was on a negative energy line, pounded stakes into the ground, moved the line, and the room was OK after that.[13]

He was something of a guru in Steamboat Springs, and he was convinced that strong energy lines came off the ridge of Woodchuck Hill.[14] For Tolles, earth energy had educational value. In the late 1980s he built a maze on the hill above the college called "The Cretan Labyrinth," and new students who arrived in the autumn walked through the maze to get "centered."

Imagine a freshman coming to an open-admission community college in a small Rocky Mountain town and being encouraged to walk through a maze because "the maze offers you a single path, from the outer world to the world within. Running the maze gets you out of your rational mind and into the here-and-now." Tolles was a college teacher in the liberal arts tradition, a tradition that emphasized that you were not in college just to learn, but to learn in such a manner that would add to your development as a person and to your future flourishing in society. For Tolles, teaching was a kind of "soulcraft."[15] Although the idea is now passé and ridiculed, in the 1980s the idea that a liberal arts/ humanities teacher could function as a secular shaman or a priest, mentoring young people toward a satisfying intellectual and personal life, was not seen as absurd.

George Tolles became my mentor at the Alpine Campus. Our teaching techniques were different—Tolles was a master of the lecture then discussion approach, while I liked the Socratic method of dialogue. Tolles often told me that the ideal college atmosphere was to have a diverse faculty with different teaching styles. I started teaching at the Alpine Campus in 1984. In 1985-1986 I took over some history courses,

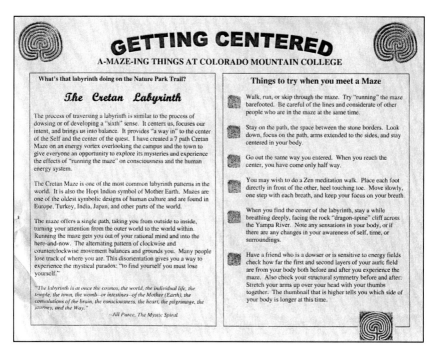

GETTING CENTERED
A-MAZE-ING THINGS AT COLORADO MOUNTAIN COLLEGE

What's that labyrinth doing on the Nature Park Trail?

The Cretan Labyrinth

The process of traversing a labyrinth is similar to the process of dowsing or of developing a "sixth" sense. It centers us, focuses our intent, and brings us into balance. It provides "a way in" to the center of the Self and the center of the quest. I have created a 7 path Cretan Maze on an energy vortex overlooking the campus and the town to give everyone an opportunity to explore its mysteries and experience the effects of "running the maze" on consciousness and the human energy system.

The Cretan Maze is one of the most common labyrinth patterns in the world. It is also the Hopi Indian symbol of Mother Earth. Mazes are one of the oldest symbolic designs of human culture and are found in Europe, Turkey, India, Japan, and other parts of the world.

The maze offers a single path, taking you from outside to inside, turning your attention from the outer world to the world within. Running the maze gets you out of your rational mind and into the here-and-now. The alternating pattern of clockwise and counterclockwise movement balances and grounds you. Many people lose track of where you are. This disorientation gives you a way to experience the mystical paradox: "to find yourself you must lose yourself."

"The labyrinth is at once the cosmos, the world, the individual life, the temple, the town, the womb–or intestines–of the Mother (Earth), the convolutions of the brain, the consciousness, the heart, the pilgrimage, the journey, and the Way."

–Jill Purce, The Mystic Spiral

Things to try when you meet a Maze

Walk, run, or skip through the maze. Try "running" the maze barefooted. Be careful of the lines and considerate of other people who are in the maze at the same time.

Stay on the path, the space between the stone borders. Look down, focus on the path, arms extended to the sides, and stay centered in your body.

Go out the same way you entered. When you reach the center, you have come only half way.

You may wish to do a Zen meditation walk. Place each foot directly in front of the other, heel touching toe. Move slowly, one step with each breath, and keep your focus on your breath.

When you find the center of the labyrinth, stay a while breathing deeply, facing the rock "dragon-spine" cliff across the Yampa River. Note any sensations in your body, or if there are any changes in your awareness of self, time, or surroundings.

Have a friend who is a dowser or is sensitive to energy fields check how far the first and second layers of your auric field are from your body both before and after you experience the maze. Also check your structural symmetry before and after: Stretch your arms up over your head with your thumbs together. The thumbnail that is higher tells you which side of your body is longer at this time.

"Getting Centered" handout. Permission from George Tolles. In the personal collection of Robert P. Baker.

and also started teaching philosophy courses. In 1987 George Bagwell told me that he "wanted a little liveliness on the campus" and gave me a permanent position.

I immediately bonded with the Lincoln Jones buildings. They were themselves labyrinths on the inside and never failed to give one the sense of the uncanny. In Willett Hall the dorm rooms were converted into small classrooms of odd shapes, requiring classes to be restricted to less than twenty students. Students were always in close but strange proximity to the teacher. Even the larger, middle classroom was small by today's standards, with places for about thirty students. All the offices were the same size, whether you were campus dean or a lowly adjunct.

In the Lincoln Jones buildings faculty, administrators, secretaries, grounds crew workers, and students were close to one another physically, and there was an easy intellectual and social atmosphere. It was a true "Community of Scholars."[16] Tolles encouraged team teaching that

Robert P. Baker teaching in Willett Hall in the 1980s. Photo by Walter Gallacher, permission granted. In the personal collection of Robert P. Baker.

allowed the faculty to sample each other's teaching techniques and learn from them. When two professors are learning together and including students in this learning process, there is an aura of electricity in the classroom that infects everybody.

My first experience was teaching world politics with Tolles. Of my other colleagues in the 1980s and 1990s I think about the late Craig Hadden, who wrote a master's thesis on John Fowles' novel, *The Magus*, and was himself something of one, and with whom I team taught classes on literature and history.[17] Hadden would get up every day at 4 a.m. and grade papers, putting more comments on them than the students had originally written. His knowledge of literature was prodigious, and his teaching severe and to the point. Together we used something like the "good cop, bad cop" approach in the classroom to great effect. I also taught courses with Paul Biagi, who had a doctorate in physics from the University of Colorado and combined a deep knowledge of quantum physics with philosophy and art.[18] I inaugurated and taught a course called "Wilderness and the American Ethic" to combine my interest in history with that of ecology and social change. In the 1990s I team taught this course with the outdoor education professor, John Saunders, who gave me a deeper appreciation of ecology and sustainability. Teaching at the Alpine Campus was always a combination of theory and practice, much like that described by the Massachusetts Institute of Technology Professor of Sustainability John R. Ehrenfeld:

> Think about our shared experiences as student and teacher. I learned with the students. They learned with me. I was their "teacher" because that was the role that I was playing, the identity I was enacting. But that didn't necessarily mean that I always knew more than they did: it didn't necessarily mean that I was smarter. It meant only that I probably had more experience.[19]

George Tolles brought another aspect of liberal arts education to the Alpine Campus that originated with Lucy Bogue: the emphasis on international studies and foreign language. Despite the pressure from the central office in Glenwood Springs to curtail the teaching of foreign languages because enrollments were not large enough, that teaching continued at the Alpine Campus. (See Table 1.)

For many in its resort communities, CMC had the reputation of "See Me Ski," and they characterized the students as underachievers who only wanted to smoke dope and be ski bums. They did not understand what happened in our classrooms. Because we had small classes, often less than fifteen students, the faculty became expertly skilled at what we called "the hook." Since Colorado Mountain College was an open-admission college, students often came in with poor high-school grades. A large number were from wealthy families but had been the objects of neglect. In 1983 Howard Gardner, a professor at Harvard University, developed the idea of multiple intelligences—seven different ways in which people learned. Many of our students came to the mountains because they loved outdoor activities, and we added an eighth intelligence that Gardner later acknowledged: "nature smart."[20] We combined academic

Table 1. *Foreign languages taught at the Alpine Campus, compiled from Colorado Mountain College Alpine Campus bulletins, 1981-2000.*

	Spanish	French	German	Italian	Japanese	Other
1981	X	X	X			
1982	X	X	X			
1983	X		X	X		
1984	X	X	X			
1985	X		X		X	
1986	X	X	X	X	X	
1987	X	X	X	X		Gaelic
1988	X	X	X			
1989	X	X	X			
1990	X	X	X	X		
1991	X	X	X			
1992		X	X	X		Chinese
1993	X	X	X		X	
1994	X	X	X		X	
1995	X	X	X		X	
1996	X	X			X	
1997	X	X	X		X	
1998	X	X	X		X	
1999	X	X			X	
2000	X	X			X	

with experiential education; the vocational educators at Alpine Campus worked closely with the academic professors, particularly Chuck Hull in ski business and John Saunders in outdoor education. We used these different approaches to "hook" the students back into an intellectual life.

In the eighteen- to twenty-one-year time of life, an important aspect of education is not to just teach facts but to encourage passion for learning and critical thinking. It is especially pernicious when teaching freshmen and sophomores to slavishly follow a lesson plan or some state-sponsored list of facts that must be learned. What is important is to raise problems that "grab" the student and allow him or her to take the issue and run with it into the realm of critical thinking. Of course this cannot be done in large lecture classes, but it is entirely possible in classes of fifteen students or less. One of my students from the late 1980s put it this way:

My favorite memory from CMC is from a Philosophy class with Bob Baker. The six of us were sitting in a circle discussing the responsibilities of humanity. I remember the depth of the conversations, the feeling of connections and the profound belief that what each of us had to say mattered, really mattered. I learned that day that I personally would make an impact, for good or ill, and that I had to actively choose to be a force for good in the world. Words can't quite express the sense of noble, enlivening responsibilities that were kindled that day, yet it was an archetypal moment of entering adulthood that has shaped my life.[21]

In the 1980s and 1990s the Alpine Campus of Colorado Mountain College, under the influence of George Tolles, practiced the following educational philosophy for the students' first two years of college:

1. Small classroom populations were to be the norm. This is where architecture and education meet; the Lincoln Jones buildings necessitated small classes.
2. A diverse and interesting faculty who combined teaching and soulcraft.
3. Faculty was to be left alone with minimal administrative interference.
4. Team teaching was encouraged.
5. Adjunct faculty were extensively mentored by the full-time faculty and treated like colleagues.
6. Classes in many foreign languages were encouraged, even if they had a very small enrollment.
7. A strong remedial education program was instituted.
8. An atmosphere of politeness and respect was demanded.
9. Continual dialogue between faculty, administrators, and support staff was encouraged.

Between 1982 and 1995 one of the most important educational experiments in America was attempted on the Alpine Campus of Colorado Mountain College. While liberal arts education in America was elitist and getting more expensive, reserved for the wealthy or meritorious few, on CMC's Alpine Campus, an open-admission college, students were treated to an elite education at bargain basement prices— the true democratic ideal of Thomas Jefferson. (See Table 2.)

Table 2. *Cost of a two semester education (30 credit hours) at the Alpine Campus of Colorado Mountain College (does not include dormitory or student fees). (Numbers in parentheses: 2013 dollars.) Compiled from Colorado Mountain College Alpine Campus bulletins, 1981-2000.*

	In District	In State	Out of State
1981	240 (594)	519 (1110)	1770 (3840)
1982	255 (522)	540 (1100)	1890 (4410)
1983	255 (576)	540 (1220)	1890 (4270)
1984	345 (747)	765 (1660)	2835 (6140)
1985	435 (909)	1005 (2100)	3555 (7430)
1986	450 (924)	1050 (2100)	3750 (7700)
1987	540 (1070)	1110 (2200)	3750 (7430)
1988	600 (1140)	1110 (2110)	4020 (7640)
1989	600 (1090)	1110 (2010)	4020 (7390)
1990	750 (1290)	1350 (2320)	4500 (7740)
1991	750 (1240)	1350 (2230)	4500 (7430)
1992	750 (1200)	1500 (2400)	4650 (7460)
1993	900 (1400)	1650 (2570)	4950 (7710)
1994	900 (1370)	1770 (2690)	5395 (8040)
1995	960 (1420)	1845 (2720)	5700 (8410)
1996	1005 (1440)	1890 (2710)	5925 (8490)
1997	1020 (1430)	1890 (2650)	6000 (8410)
1998	1080 (1490)	1920 (2650)	6150 (8490)
1999	1140 (1540)	1950 (2630)	6300 (8510)
2000	1170 (1580)	1965 (2650)	6375 (8610)

Associate of arts graduates from the Alpine Campus transferred to four-year colleges, both public and private, all over the country. Many then went on to get graduate degrees. Alpine Campus also became the most successful of all the Colorado Mountain College locations; George Tolles remembers that at district-wide meetings there was a fear that the Alpine Campus would overwhelm the rest of the college.[22] At district meetings in Glenwood Springs, the Alpine faculty was sneeringly taunted as thinking that we were the "Harvard on the Yampa." That intended insult was a vindication of our teaching efforts. By 1993 Alpine Campus had 350 full-time students, evenly divided between those wanting to transfer to four-year colleges and those who were in vocational programs such as ski business and resort management. The campus could have admitted many more students, but dorm space in existing buildings was limited. The buildings that Lincoln Jones designed were necessary, but no longer sufficient.

Bristol Hall

WHEN NEW BUILDINGS ARE CONSTRUCTED on their campuses, there are varying levels of faculty involvement. The usual pattern is to have a meeting with faculty before the architectural plans are complete, and the administrators ask for faculty suggestions. After that the architects, builders, and administration carry on the construction process, and often the resulting building is quite different from the one the faculty thought they were getting. When the Lincoln Jones buildings were planned for Woodchuck Hill in 1965, the faculty was not involved in the process: Robert Pietrowski and Lincoln Jones simply decided on the architectural plans and found a local builder. During the construction of Bristol Hall on Woodchuck Hill in 1993, the opposite scenario occurred: there was faculty involvement in almost every phase of the construction.

By 1993 George Bagwell had gone back to teaching and John Vickery was the dean of Alpine Campus. Vickery was born near Lincoln, Nebraska, in 1942. He attended the University of Nebraska in Lincoln, dropped out for a time to serve in the U.S. Navy, and finally graduated with a degree in business administration; he later received a master's degree in economics. He found a job teaching at the Leadville Campus of the still young Colorado Mountain College. He later transferred to the CMC district office in Glenwood Springs and eventually became curriculum director for the college. When the college was reorganized

John Vickery. From *Alpine Campus Yearbook,*
1990. Archives, Steamboat Springs Campus,
Copyright Colorado Mountain College.

in 1982, George Bagwell brought him to Steamboat Springs as assistant dean.

Although Vickery was more interested in business and economics courses, he balanced the academic and vocational programs at the campus. Liberal arts remained the "cadillac program" of Alpine Campus. More importantly, he had good relations with the district office. Vickery teamed with Ed Hill, a banker in Steamboat Springs and president of the CMC board of trustees, to put pressure on the district office for a new building on Alpine Campus.

The procedure for planning and constructing educational buildings had changed considerably between 1964 and 1993. Gone were the days when Lucy Bogue could bring Victor Hornbein from Denver or Robert Pietrowski could stroll down Lincoln Avenue and drop into Lincoln Jones' office. Individual architects were now subordinate to large architectural companies. In 1991 the district office formed a building committee and sent out requests for proposals for a 40,000 square foot building with a budget of $5 million to architectural firms. Rick Avery, the building supervisor at the district office, chose the Denver architectural firm of AndersonMasonDale (AMD).[1]

In 1990 AMD designed three buildings on the University of Colorado campus in Boulder and a building for the Community College

Paul Hack. From Paul Hack, permission granted.

of Aurora. AMD said of themselves that they " . . . prided themselves on understanding the importance of site and the transforming of space into a meaningful campus place," and that they combined "a strong historicist sentiment for fitting a new building to older architecture with a modernist impulse for making a bold statement."[2]

The architect chosen by AMD to be the principle designer of the new building was Paul Hack. Hack was raised in West Babylon, New York, went to the University of Colorado at Boulder where he received a bachelor's degree in environmental design, and then went to the University of Oregon for a master's degree in architecture. His architectural work was influenced by Le Corbusier and also by his teachers, Louis Kahn and James Spelling.[3] His official biography states:

> Paul Hack has a greater faith in the iterative nature of design—the idea that the constant reinterpretation and revisiting of an idea will inform the designer and provide a

more meaningful architecture. It is the credo of the craftsman who believes that the process will always be more
revealing than the product.[4]

Hack and Vickery soon became close personal friends, and Hack
came to Steamboat Springs for many discussions with the faculty and
staff. George Tolles had just retired so other faculty members took the
lead in telling Hack about the academic orientation of Alpine Campus.
The faculty—in retrospect mistakenly—thought that Alpine Campus
could carve a niche within Colorado Mountain College as the "Harvard
on the Yampa." Hack told us that it would be a mistake for the campus
to "freeze itself" and believed that the various buildings on a campus
should both fit harmoniously together so that "the existing architectural
vocabulary be reinterpreted in a more contemporary way."[5] He caught
our enthusiasm for the liberal arts and our desire for a building that
would reflect a liberal arts education and the idea of a "community of
scholars." He thought that Alpine Campus needed to "rise up" to the
status of a "real college," and he wanted a building that would be " . . . both
unique and functional."[6] The buzzword for faculty and administration
on Alpine Campus at that time was "shared governance." Because of
the close relationship between Hack and Vickery, and because Hack's
openness to faculty ideas at every stage of the building process, plans
for the new building reflected a collaboration not often found in college
construction.

In the late 1980s and early 1990s Steamboat Springs experienced a
building boom, and the results were not altogether felicitous. Paul Hack
commented:

> Additionally, it is important to remain outside of the existing
> "ski industry" typology evident in the eastern [*sic*] part of
> town. The nature of the campus plan, set along a ridge on a
> prominent hillside suggests an "academic village" more in
> the Jeffersonian tradition; buildings are appropriately scaled,
> clearly articulated and provide a pleasant and comfortable
> fit with the natural landscape.[7]

Elevation of proposed building by AndersonMasonDale Architects. Permission granted by Paul Hack.

To minimize the effect of a giant building on Woodchuck Hill, the original design by AMD for Bristol Hall actually broke the building up into three separate sections with different rooflines, divided by stairwells and flat roofs.

In its description of the building, AMD stated:

> The most dramatic is the classroom portion of the building. Here a screen wall has been extruded from the building's façade, as if peeled away . . . Behind the screen is a bright yellow wall that changes tones with the movement of the sun. Greenhouses and balconies are integrated within the screen framework to provide a visual counter-play with the southwest façade.[8]

Hack added:

> The nature of the campus plan together with notions concerning hillside architecture suggest an approach in which the massing of buildings is broken down into smaller

View from windows of Lincoln Jones' Bogue Hall. The stairwell windows offered views of Steamboat Springs and Mount Werner, and were reminiscent of Frank Lloyd Wright's Freeman House of 1923 in Los Angeles. Photo by Ken Proper.

scale elements. The value of this massing strategy becomes evident as one approaches the campus from town. Although a highly visible, figurative building might be desirable when viewed from a distance, care should be taken to scale the

View from Paul Hack's Bristol Hall. The stairwell windows were designed to make a historicist connection to the older buildings designed by Lincoln Jones. Photo by Ken Proper.

building to fit comfortably with the surrounding residential context.[9]

For Paul Hack, the new multi-purpose building would not only fit the site and give a strong image to the community, but also have good solar orientation. The windows in the stairwells were designed to make a historicist connection to the older buildings designed by Lincoln Jones.

The internal configuration of the building was the subject of many meetings between faculty, staff, and administration that continued right through the construction process. Unlike most other new college architecture in the United States at this time, all of the offices—faculty and administration—were made the same size—10 feet by 10 feet. The middle classroom building had one large lecture hall, but the rest of the classrooms were kept deliberately small. The small classrooms at the back of the ground floor were without windows and rather depressing.[10] On the third floor Hack designed a very welcoming library. The halls of the building were decorated with pillars and sconces so that the walls could become places for art and the building would avoid a prison-like inner appearance.

The main entrance had a high ceiling where an imaginative sculpture could be hung. Faculty offices were in the west building where the faculty members could communicate easily with one another, and the space was designed with an outside balcony where faculty could congregate in good weather. The east section was an auditorium and gymnasium.

The idealistic visions of Paul Hack and the faculty at Alpine Campus were never quite realized. It was discovered that the $5 million budgeted by the district office for construction was for a metal, Butler-type building, and the budget for the Paul Hack design required an additional $2 million, something Vickery and Ed Hill were able to wrestle out of the board of trustees. Even then the design was too expensive, so the three separate buildings with the stairwells between them, the most unique part of Hack's design, became a single-barrel, vaulted roof, thus making the building more monolithic and increasing its impact on Woodchuck Hill. As the building neared completion, cost overruns of $100,000 occurred. Bill Gauthier, the vice president for finances at the district office, urged that the building be mothballed. Vickery had to make some tough decisions. Brick facing, a historicist motif that would have tied the new building aesthetically to the existing buildings designed by Lincoln Jones was scrapped in favor of bare concrete and a new science lab. The

View of completed Bristol Hall hallway. Photo by Ken Proper.

greenhouse was abandoned; cheap chairs and tables were chosen for the interior. The balcony for the faculty offices was made smaller and constructed out of cheap steel.[11]

When the Lincoln Jones buildings appeared on Woodchuck Hill, even in their strangeness they excited little controversy. Before building the Paul Hack structure, the college had presented the plans for the building to the public and held a series of town meetings, with very little comment from the community.[12] But after construction the completed building incited wide-scale outrage. The bare concrete walls were seen as ugly, and the yellow color as "a garish intrusion on the landscape."[13] There were angry letters to the editor in the *Steamboat Pilot*, and a community organization sent the college a critical letter—John Vickery remembers it as "nasty."[14]

After much agonizing, Vickery assembled a community committee that included Steamboat Springs architect Robert S. Ralston. The committee recommended that a red stucco finish should be put on the concrete blocks and that the yellow should be painted over. (See Ken Proper's before and after photographs of Bristol Hall on the back cover.)

What remained was to name the building. John Vickery remembers that there was strong pressure on him to sell the naming rights, but he insisted on a historicist connection to the educational traditions of Woodchuck Hill.[15] Olive Morton, dean of community education, asked the Steamboat Springs community for suggestions to be submitted in writing "with a short explanation of the reasons for a suggested name."[16] The community submitted many suggestions. Bill Hill recommended John Fetcher; John Whittum suggested Charlotte Perry. The final decision favored Ev Bristol, whose name, according to Colorado Mountain College President Dennis Mayer at the dedication of the building " . . . is etched in the history of this unique campus."[17] It was decided that the faculty wing of Bristol Hall be named after Professor Emeritus George Tolles who, Mayer said, " . . . is almost as much an institution as the college itself."

The completed building was not without its problems. The tight budget restricted the size of the gym and prohibited a locker room. Classrooms had lower ceilings and zone heating instead of thermostats in every room. The metal studs meant that sounds in one room could be heard in another. Heavy doors into the faculty wing made access difficult for students. Administrators were not entirely pleased with their small offices. The most serious problem came with winter snow. If the Lincoln Jones designed flat-roof buildings leaked from built-up snow, in the AMD design snow came hurtling off the roof in dangerous amounts.[18] After the first year, AMD designed snow bars to hold the snow on the roof, but that only caused even more snow to come down. After several years, without consulting architect Paul Hack, ugly "doghouses" were placed at the front and back entrances to keep snow from falling on people entering the building. Later, the atrium was eliminated in favor of an upstairs student lounge.

AMD proposed a creative campus plan based on the "crescent linear" model that followed the contour of Woodchuck Hill from west to north. At the end of the crescent there would be an events field and amphitheater.

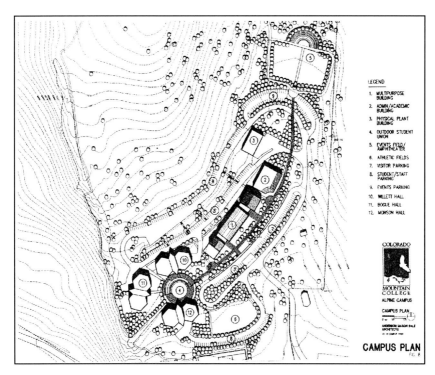

Colorado Mountain College Alpine Campus Plan by AndersonMasonDale Architects. The plan was never fully realized. Courtesy of Planning Commission, City of Steamboat Springs, Colorado. Permission granted by Paul Hack.

Below Monson Hall would be an athletic field. A pedestrian path would link the various parts of the campus. None of this ever happened.

Physical plant buildings were eventually added to the campus, but instead of being architecturally compatible with the existing buildings, they were metal, industrial-type structures. The administrator who over-saw buildings for the district office and who was not, in Vickery's words, a "person of process," never discussed his plans for a maintenance building with the Alpine Campus faculty and staff. He just came to Steamboat Springs and supervised its construction. The result was an unfortunate modification to the view of the main building as seen from the town.

Further around the hill, Paul Hack had envisaged an events field and amphitheater. Instead, a new residence hall named for Bill Hill and Ed Hill was constructed in 1996.[19] It was a "cookie cutter" building, designed by

Aerial view of Colorado Mountain College Alpine Campus in the 1990s. Photo by George Bagwell, permission granted.

the firm of Gustafson in Aspen, one of three similar buildings placed on the three residential Colorado Mountain College campuses and actually copied from the community college in Meeker. No thought was given to make it fit the existing architecture of the campus or the contours of Woodchuck Hill. Both John Vickery and Brian Hoza, the dean of student services on Alpine Campus, were excluded from the decision-making process. Hoza was familiar with recent trends in dormitories that emphasized more familial living spaces of small pods, but he was not consulted.[20] Instead, Alpine Campus received a building that looked like a motel on the outside and a prison inside. From lack of foresight, it was built over an underground stream without adequate French drains, causing some first floor rooms to flood at certain times of the year and mold to grow up the walls. However, it did establish Alpine Campus as a residential center and allow for an increase in enrollment. For the time being, Alpine Campus was complete.

The Academic Center

ON A BEAUTIFUL AUTUMN DAY in 2011 George Bagwell looked out of his third-floor office window in Bristol Hall and gave a huge sigh of relief—the first shovelfuls of soil for a new building had been scooped out just beneath his window. He said to me, "Now they cannot take away our campus on Woodchuck Hill." Bagwell had been on Woodchuck Hill since 1982, and he knew from firsthand experience the various attempts by the Colorado Mountain College district office in Glenwood Springs during the past thirty years to curtail and even eliminate Alpine Campus in Steamboat Springs. He also knew that in the past many in the district office and at the commuter campuses thought that community colleges should not support residential campuses.

In 2008 Stan Jensen, the new president of Colorado Mountain College, chose Peter A. Perhac as vice president of the college and CEO of Alpine Campus.[1] Perhac was a vocational specialist, having spent most of his career in colleges of medicine, and he had no experience with community colleges. He was the product of the Catholic Jesuit educational system, having graduated from a private Catholic high school, gone to college for bachelor's and master's degrees from John Carroll College, and finally receiving a doctorate from San Francisco University. He described himself as the consummate administrator, and said that he "came down" to the community college level in order to "sample every type of higher education" and to become "administratively" well-rounded."[2]

Peter Perhac in 2008.
Courtesy of *Steamboat Today* Photo Archives.
Photo by John F. Russell.

In 2009-2010 Colorado Mountain College had an opportunity to change the entrance to Alpine Campus. The existing entrance on 12th Street was difficult to find and navigate. That entrance was made possible by an easement given to the college in 1980 by David Combs, who bought land for a subdivision on Woodchuck Hill. There was a second easement into Woodchuck Hill, from Crawford Avenue, that John Fetcher obtained from Steamboat Springs when he sold the college land to William Rust of United States International University in 1968. But access through Crawford Avenue would not meet code and would require costly widening. CMC was already planning a new building for Woodchuck Hill, and a new, more attractive entrance to the campus was considered as a possibility. Harry Dike, who owned property below the college on U.S. Highway 40, wanted to sell his land to the college so that a new entrance road could come directly off Lincoln Avenue.[3] Dike was willing to sell the parcel to CMC for $4 million, of which he would donate $500,000 back to the college. On September 7, 2010, in preparation for the city council meeting of September 9, H+L Architects of Denver sent the city planning commission a drawing of what the road would look like.

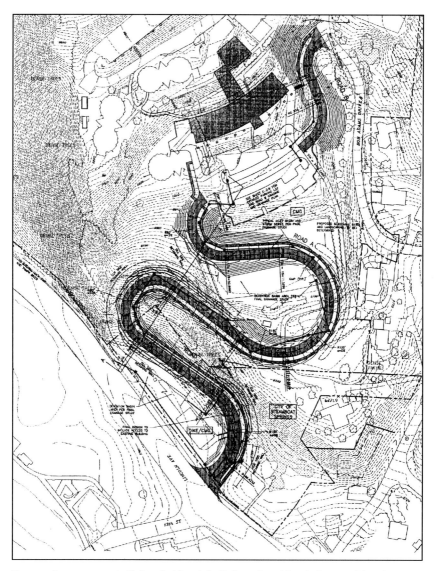

Proposed new access to Colorado Mountain College from Lincoln Avenue. The plan was
never realized. Courtesy of Planning Commission, City of Steamboat Springs, Colorado.
Permission granted by H+L Architects. Copyright Colorado Mountain College.

On September 9, 2010, President Jensen and Facilities Manager Sam
Skramstad from the district office appeared before the Steamboat Springs
city council to discuss the Dike property entrance that would create an

intersection at Highway 40 and 13th Street. After much discussion, the council decided to support a variance for a right turn lane on Highway 40, but requested the college to do further traffic studies.[4] Stan Jensen exploded. He said that Colorado Mountain College was trying to be a partner with the city, but it was not in the road business and would not spend any more money on additional studies.[5] He threatened to move CMC out of Steamboat Springs if the city did not support the college.[6]

In September and October of 2010 Colorado Mountain College gave the impression that it was seriously considering leaving Woodchuck Hill. The night before closing, the Dikes heard a rumor that CMC representatives would not show up. When they went to the closing, the college officials did not appear.[7] At that point Jensen sent Peter Perhac to real-estate agents in order to scout for land to buy west of town for a new campus.[8] Whether Jensen and Perhac were serious or just posturing is an open question.[9] Either way, pressure was now put on the city to allow the college to use the Crawford Avenue easement as the road for the new building and to modify some of the code requirements.[10] On October 18 Jensen sent a letter to the city stating that the college would not accept any intergovernmental agreement between CMC and the city. On October 25 CMC sent a memo to the city, written by Skramstad, requesting that the Crawford Spur at 12th Street be approved as the access road.[11] In January 2011 the city council retreated before Jensen's threats, who again stated, "It is a possibility that CMC would leave this community and money is an issue."[12]

The Dike access would have given the college a separate and more appealing entrance off Highway 40 and a more attractive campus. Some people in Steamboat Springs, such as architect Robert S. Ralston, thought the college missed a historical opportunity to develop a more appealing campus for Woodchuck Hill. He told city council, "You all had it right when you had the 13th Street entrance to the college . . . that was good long-term planning . . . I think we're rushing into a lot of stuff here you may regret." Although many in the audience spoke against the ordinance and the Crawford Spur, city council approved the termination of the older intergovernmental agreement between Steamboat Springs and the college.[13] Colorado Mountain College could now do whatever it wanted on Woodchuck Hill without any city interference.

After the year 2000, Colorado Mountain College began an ambitious building program on its three campuses and eight centers.[14] Discussions for Steamboat Springs, the last campus to get a new building, began in 2009, just as the economic crisis in the United States was becoming apparent. George Bagwell proposed that the first construction be for an addition to the residence hall so that more students could live on campus, and then a second building for residence hall support. Later would come a vocational education building, a classroom building, an auditorium that would also be a concert hall, and a planetarium. For this building, Bagwell envisaged a community partnership for first-class performance venues, a hall large enough to accommodate graduation, and a planetarium that would operate when concerts were not scheduled. He wanted this hall to be located as low as possible on Woodchuck Hill so it would be pedestrian friendly. He was thinking of the construction needed for growing campus enrollments and for the Woodchuck Hill tradition of a liberal arts residential college tied closely to the vocational programs and the community.[15] Bagwell's suggestions were ignored.

For the new building at the Alpine Campus, the college put out a call for bids for a 52,000 square foot building that was to cost $18 million. Five firms bid on the project and the bid was given to H+L Architects, although H+L was not the lowest bidder. Peter Perhac had experience in overseeing new college construction in his previous jobs so he was seen as well qualified to manage the construction. He told me that the college chose H+L because they proposed a financially viable budget and had good educational experience, and he was impressed with the buildings the firm had designed at the University of Colorado.[16] Perhac consulted with the faculty at the beginning of the planning process, but there was little faculty involvement once construction began.

Even more than in 1993, educational construction had become infinitely more complicated. Unlike the Lincoln Jones buildings or Paul Hack's Bristol Hall, H+L did not feature any one architect. Chad Novak of H+L put it this way:

I was the lead designer and actually was the architect who
gave the presentations at city council meetings. However, as
you know on projects of this magnitude, "it takes a village"
and the entire H+L Architecture team deserves equal credit.
We all have our area of expertise, mine is to set the big idea
and develop the design concept. Ariel [Madlambayan] is the
detail and design development man, and Nick McCormick
and Rob Biesk were instrumental in the construction
coordination.[17]

Ariel Madlambayan was the spokesman for H+L when he appeared
before the city planning commission in February 2011, using plural
pronouns:

We wanted to create a building that fitted into the hillside.
This will be a three-story structure. We want a more rustic
look to it. There's stone throughout the facility, brick on
some of the major wing walls, metal panel roof system, and
metal panel elements along the wall. The colors are more
earth toned to help it not stand out on that hillside.[18]

For the Alpine Campus, H+L Architects looked at Woodchuck
Hill and thought about several alternatives that they called slide, shift,
spin, and signal. Their final proposal was a synthesis of the shift and
spin that sited the new building below the existing Bristol Hall, kept the
three Lincoln Jones buildings, and called for the new entrance road into
the college. This was a variation of the upper/lower campus originally
designed by Victor Hornbein in 1965.

In early 2011 plans for the building were enlarged to 69,000 square
feet, and the estimated cost increased to $22.9 million. The building
had been originally designed for expansion in the future, but Colorado
Mountain College decided to expand it because, according to H+L
Architects, "a full build out [would] capitalize on the cost savings of
adding it in the initial construction phase versus at a later date when cost
would like be higher."[19] The expanded building would now require the

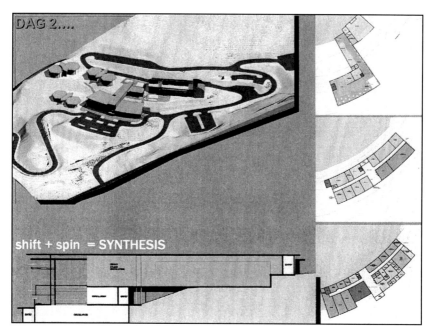

Proposed plans by H+L Architecture for the new building on Woodchuck Hill. Note that the Lincoln Jones buildings are still part of the campus and that the proposed building does not dominate hill. Courtesy of Planning Commission, City of Steamboat Springs, Colorado.

demolition of Monson Hall, the original 1966 Lincoln Jones building, and of all his buildings on Woodchuck Hill, the one in the poorest physical condition.

Construction was both complicated and expensive, with a roster of structural engineers, HVAC (heating, ventilation, air conditioning) specialists, interior designers, computer software engineers, and environmental impact managers. Every week Peter Perhac convened a meeting of the principle players—representatives of Adolfson & Peterson Construction; a representative from ARC Integrated Program Management Inc. to oversee the financial details; a representative from H+L Architects; the local architect representing H+L; someone from Civil Design Consultants for geological engineering; and of course, representatives from Colorado Mountain College. This is where Perhac did the job for which he was hired; he was clearly the boss who kept all of the construction and engineering and finances moving in the same direction.[20] He was aided by the weather—a mild winter in Steamboat Springs without much snow.

Because the new building was lower and wider than Bristol Hall, over 9,000 cubic yards of fill was brought in and held in place by a new technology of "vibratory replacement stone aggregate columns." Springs and underground rivers on the hill necessitated an elaborate system of French drains to be placed under the building, with a holding pond to be built below. The building is technologically sophisticated. Fifty-six geothermal wells 500 feet deep were drilled under the building: water is circulated through these wells, heated by the below ground temperature and brought up to the surface and returned by an elaborate system of electric pumps. A computerized heating and cooling system circulates the proper air temperature (the building has no windows that open) in both summer and winter. There are backup systems in case some aspect of the heating and cooling fails and a special fire room in case of a larger catastrophe. By and large, the building was constructed on time and within the budget of $23 million.[21]

The building is called the "Academic Center" and it does contain a few large classrooms. However, it is actually a modern administrative, vocational, and entertainment building that portrays Colorado Mountain College as successful and thriving. The ideas of the architect Paul Hack— who in 1993 wanted a liberal arts building on Woodchuck Hill that would be "appropriately scaled," not mimic existing buildings in Steamboat Springs or resort towns, and show that Alpine Campus had attained the status of a "real college"—were all reversed in 2012. From the standpoint of public relations these reversals were warranted: unlike Bristol Hall, the Academic Center has been widely welcomed by the community. The Steamboat Springs building has strong resemblances to high-school buildings that H+L designed for the nearby towns of Gypsum and Edwards. H+L described their buildings in the mountains of Colorado as "derived from the context of the community and Sense of Place that one has when in those environments . . . Mountain environments are rich with views and vistas from which we try to capture and frame in

Academic Center front entrance stairway. Photo by Ken Proper.

inspiring ways. Expanses of glass that capture the views from key public zones enhance the connection to the environment."[22]

The entrance is quite stunning in an industrial sense. One walks into a large open space with exposed heating pipes and a long stairway going up two stories. It gives the feeling of raw power.[23]

On the first floor, to the right of the stairway are administrative offices and offices of Steamboat Springs businesses; on the left are exercise and yoga/pilates rooms and rooms for ski tuning, plus the pumps for the thermal heat and an emergency safety room. On the second floor, again to the right, are administrative offices and offices for vocational faculty. The administrative offices feature a large open space and conference room. The largest office —a corner office—is for the vice president of the college. Across from the faculty offices is an art studio. To the right are large classrooms, designed to teach forty students in lecture situations.

The walls are bare and stark: no art is allowed—and in this part of the building the hallways remind one of a factory for the production of students in the post-industrial society.

Hallway in the Academic Center. Photo by Ken Proper.

The third floor is the most impressive because of the architectural use of "empty space" to create large open areas. There is a snack bar with places for students to relax, and a "bookstore" that no longer carries books.[24] A large cafeteria and a conference-restaurant overlook the Yampa Valley, and a balcony provides a wonderful view of Steamboat Springs. There is a culinary section with, it has been rumored, over a million dollars of equipment for the new culinary program, now another "cadillac program" of the Alpine Campus.[25]

Above the third floor and toward Bristol Hall is an auditorium. It is quite small, only having a 200-person capacity because a larger auditorium would have required more exits and fire regulations. The small size means that graduation ceremonies or events that could unite the whole student body cannot be held there. The auditorium is really for large lecture classes or smaller concerts and dance events.

Dining area in Academic Center. Photo by Ken Proper.

The Lincoln Jones buildings of 1966 were named after supporters of education in Steamboat Springs: Lucy Bogue, Ray Monson, Dr. Willett. In 1993 Bristol Hall was named following a public referendum in which citizens of Steamboat Springs were encouraged to nominate their favorite supporters of higher education. In the new 2012 building, every room, every hall, every nook and cranny is named for whomever can give Colorado Mountain College the most money. George Bagwell, who more than any other person is responsible for the success of Alpine Campus, had to buy his own plaque—which was placed in the kitchen of the faculty coffee nook! There is no reference to former Dean John Vickery, also responsible for the success of the campus. The money raised, possibly $2 million added to the $23 million building fund, helped pay for the desks and furnishings.[26] The message to the students is clear—everything in education is for sale. "No money, no mission." At the time of this writing no one has come up with the million dollars asked to name the entire building, and it remains the Academic Center.

Because of its size and the views from its windows, the building could be called "inspiring." Nothing in the architecture of the Academic Center suggests a historicist link to Woodchuck Hill. You could easily mistake it for the offices of an investment firm or an insurance company.[27] A pleasant and welcoming building with stunning vistas now dominates Woodchuck Hill. There is little architectural sense of the uncanny. But—and George Bagwell reminds me of this every time I see him—the building guarantees that a college campus will endure on Woodchuck Hill.

A Minority of One

WHEN I DISCOVERED IN 2010 that Colorado Mountain College had decided to demolish all of the Lincoln Jones buildings from the 1960s, I was stunned. Those uncanny buildings had stood guard on Woodchuck Hill for almost fifty years. I naively thought that even the most vocational administrators would have some feeling for the liberal arts historical traditions of Woodchuck Hill, that the faculty would rise up against the demolition, that the historic preservation community of Steamboat Springs would exert its weight, that the architects would protect the memory of one of their own, that the City of Steamboat Springs would be interested in preserving its history, that at least a few citizens of the town would protest. But there was little response. I felt like a minority of one, although I have since discovered that a few others felt the same way. I determined to write a history of those lost buildings as part of a larger history of the architecture on Woodchuck Hill.

The first question I asked was who was responsible for the decision to demolish those buildings. That should seem an easy question to answer. Colorado Mountain College is a public institution with tax-collecting powers controlled by a seven-member board of trustees. Each member represents a different school district and is elected by a vote from that district. The Steamboat Springs school district elects one member of the board. However, this does not answer the question. Educational

111

CMC Steamboat
Willett Cost Allowances

Updated: 20SEP11

Scope Description	Cost	Notes
Property Conditions Assessment & Energy Audit	$ 20,000.00	To determine upgrades required to Willett
Traffic Study	$ 12,000.00	Increased campus sq. footage requires traffic study
Additional Parking Lot, Design & Construction	$ 250,000.00	Location for additional parking is unknown; cost dependent on site & required amount of parking spaces
Full Sprinklering of Willett	$ 350,000.00	
Return Water Fee Credit	$ 78,000.00	
Hydraulic Analysis	$ 15,000.00	Required per City of Steamboat if campus sq. footage increases; determine if water main size is adequate
Increase main gas line to 4"	$ 50,000.00	
Historic Preservation of Willett	$ 50,000.00	Range could be $20,000 - $200,000 depending on requirements
Redesign delivery access to kitchen	$ 20,000.00	
Redesign exits & entrances on 2nd floor	$ 75,000.00	
Replace bathroom floors	$ 25,000.00	
Replace carpet	$ 100,000.00	Assumes 10-15,000 sq. ft
Replace Roof	$ 200,000.00	Will depend on amount of insulation that needs replaced
Replace elevator	$ 100,000.00	
Add heating to 1st level bathrooms	$ 50,000.00	
Upgrade plumbing	$ 250,000.00	Assumes $10/SF
Upgrade HVAC	$ 375,000.00	Assumes $15/SF
Replace electric panel & main disconnect	$ 250,000.00	May require new xfr and new primary
Mold abatement in crawl space	$ 60,000.00	Cost based on Hill Hall abatement costs
Asbestos abatement in walls/ceiling	$ 50,000.00	
Upgrade windows	$ 75,000.00	
Replace fire panel	$ 125,000.00	Assumes $5/SF
Security Access to doors & door replacement	$ 50,000.00	
Fire rating of ceilings & walls	$ 100,000.00	Assumes $4/SF
Grease Trap	$ 10,000.00	
Design Team Allowance/Plans	$ 75,000.00	
Construction Allowance	$ 332,250.00	15%
TOTAL Cost	$ 3,147,250.00	
Potential Hwy 40 Work	$450,000	Increased size of campus may trigger traffic light & road adjustments at Hwy 40. Cost range could be $450,000 - $1.5M

"Rough Order of Magnitude" for Willett Hall. From Central Services, Colorado Mountain College, Glenwood Springs. Copyright Colorado Mountain College.

administrators at every level have told governing boards that they should have nothing to do with the actual day-to-day management of their institutions.[1] Stan Jensen was president of the college from 2008 to 2012, and Peter Perhac was dean of the Alpine Campus. These men were the de facto owners of Woodchuck Hill. They made the decision to demolish all of the Lincoln Jones buildings.[2]

Why did they make this decision? Of the three buildings, Monson Hall had to come down when Colorado Mountain College decided to increase the size of the Academic Center, and it was the Lincoln Jones building that was in the worst physical shape. The official argument for the destruction of the remaining two buildings was that they would have been too expensive to repair. The financial argument possibly would have made sense for Bogue Hall since it had some mold and asbestos, although no study was done to find out what the exact costs would be. However, the college had put more than a million dollars into Willett Hall: it had been completely remodeled in 1994, almost all of the asbestos taken out in the 1990s, and the roof repaired in 2002. Perhac told a faculty meeting that a study for Willett Hall had been undertaken and that the cost to keep Willett would be $3.1 million.[3] But no in-depth engineering assessment was ever made, and no attempt was made to contact the historic preservation assessment community. Sara Lara, representative for ARC Integrated Management (before she left the project in midstream) in September 2011 wrote a short, one-page summary of the possible costs to keep Willett, called a Rough Order of Magnitude (ROM).[4] Like most rough drafts of this sort, costs were exaggerated so as to err on the side of caution.

When the Academic Center was constructed, the Steamboat Springs fire department insisted that all buildings on campus be equipped with sprinkler systems. Only the older Lincoln Jones buildings and the maintenance buildings lacked these systems. Lara's ROM stated that the cost of "sprinklering" [sic] Willett Hall would be $350,000, and this was a figure often quoted when justifying the destruction of Willett Hall. However, when the Health and Recreation building in Steamboat Springs—also redesigned by Lincoln Jones in the 1960s and with

113

approximately the same square footage—put in sprinklers in 2012, the total cost, including digging a tap from the street, was less than half of that, $122,000.[5] If the college had decided to spend that money, Willett Hall could have been saved and slowly improved over the years. The sprinkler system was all that was necessary to save the building. Instead, the college spent nearly $500,000 to tear it down and build a parking lot.[6] The financial argument for destroying the buildings that the college administrators used made no sense, but it convinced the faculty and it hid other and more probable reasons.

A second possible reason for destruction of the Lincoln Jones buildings was related to water taps and interference by the City of Steamboat Springs. After the fiasco of the Dike entrance, the city had relinquished any right to interfere on Woodchuck Hill. However, if the college had to pay for new water and sewer taps from the city, the approval of those taps would once again give the city the power to influence decisions about buildings, landscaping, and preservation. When Hill Hall was built on Woodchuck Hill in 1996 and needed water and sewage hookups, the city, under pressure from Buckskin subdivision near the college, insisted on an intergovernmental agreement that gave the city some control over Woodchuck Hill. In 2014 the Lincoln Jones buildings would have been fifty years old, and the city's preservation officer with the planning commission was interested in them as historically important. The college wanted to avoid city interference at all costs. Lara explained, "I do remember that there were certain assumptions that needed to be made with what the City might require since the occupancy level changed greatly with keeping Willett."[7] The most interesting item in the ROM is the "Return Water Fee Credit." To avoid paying new tap fees to the city, the college transferred the taps from the existing Lincoln Jones buildings to the new building. If Willett Hall had been saved, another tap fee for the new building would have been required. The way to avoid city intervention was to transfer all three existing water taps from the three buildings, thereby saving a small amount of money and keeping the city out.

There was a third reason for destroying the Lincoln Jones buildings that had to do with a projected plan to build an upscale hotel and

Conceptual rendering of "Resort Management Teaching Hotel and Planetarium Classroom Building." Copyright Cynthia Pougiales, AIA. Permission from Thira, Inc., architect Cynthia Pougiales. Copy of rendering from Central Services, Colorado Mountain College, Glenwood Springs. Copyright Colorado Mountain College.

restaurant on Woodchuck Hill. When the Academic Center project was expanded from 52,000 to 69,000 square feet, there was already a plan to attach a walkway from the large third-floor dining room of the Academic Center to an upscale hotel and restaurant that would extend north and south along the ridge of Woodchuck Hill. For many months an architectural sketch of the new hotel was displayed in a prominent position above the door of Peter Perhac's office. It was an imaginative building on three levels that came down the hill where the Lincoln Jones buildings had stood, and its most prominent feature was the glass walkway that connected it to the Academic Center dining room. Perhac's idea was to expand the resort management program to include managing a luxury hotel with a quality restaurant that provided food prepared by culinary students. The Lincoln Jones buildings were torn down so that there would be a "blank slate" of ground for the new hotel.

When Stan Jensen left in 2012, the hotel project became moot. The new president of Colorado Mountain College has ordered the college facilities manager to write a new facilities master plan for the college, and at this writing, it is doubtful that a $17-million luxury hotel will be in that plan. The Lincoln Jones buildings were torn down for an ambitious, yet dubious, project that will probably never happen.

It had been known since 2010 that the administrators of Colorado Mountain College had decided to destroy the Lincoln Jones buildings. That was when I started my research on Jones, and I tried in every conceivable manner to get people interested in saving the buildings. Yet for two years there was little response. How could Colorado Mountain College have so easily destroyed the Lincoln Jones buildings without protest? One answer lies in contemporary attitudes toward "modern" architecture in general and to the Lincoln Jones buildings in particular. Modern architecture originated at the turn of the twentieth century, and its apogee was from the 1930s to the 1960s. It practitioners often designed buildings that were strange and struck contemporaries as difficult to understand. Because of their uncanny nature, many mid-twentieth-century modernist buildings have today become objects of scorn. Robin Pogrebin wrote in the *New York Times*:

> As Modernist buildings reach middle age, many of the stark structures that once represented the architectural vanguard are showing signs of wear, setting off debates around the country between preservationists, who see them as historical landmarks, and the many people who just see them as eyesores.[8]

Architectural conservationists—who as conservatives want to posit that " . . . before destroying things we should pause to consider their merits,"[9]—are now presented with "unprecedented challenges" by the aging landmarks of modernism.[10] Nowhere is this truer than on college campuses,[11] and nowhere was it truer than on Woodchuck Hill. The Yampa Valley College buildings of the 1960s had been conceived as part of an idealistic educational community where students lived and studied together. However, they had not been used in that manner since 1969 and were afterward neglected and then used in different ways. They were difficult to navigate for those who were new to them, and difficult to work in for those who had other purposes. Their very nature made them objects of scorn.

116

Historic preservation is usually an ethical issue: what intrinsic value do we put on the past?[12] However, it can also be supported on pragmatic grounds. George Bagwell did not think that the Lincoln Jones buildings had intrinsic value, but he did argue that they had pragmatic value, because if they were destroyed the Steamboat Springs campus would actually lose valuable classroom space needed for future development.[13]

I argued, to no avail, that the buildings had intrinsic value. They were historic because they had stood over Steamboat Springs for almost fifty years. They were an outstanding example of mid-century modern architecture as it had developed in Boulder, and had spread to the Western Slope. They symbolized the long liberal arts tradition of Woodchuck Hill.

As the twentieth century morphed into the twenty-first, I found myself looking at the buildings with a new appreciation that originated from an assessment of today's high-speed life. We now live in a frantic world of overwhelming speed characterized by a recent writer as "mind-numbing simultaneity and a frantic realm of homogenized instantaneity, synchronic depthlessness and undifferentiated closure."[14] High modernism in art and architecture is customarily associated with speed, acceleration, and ceaseless movement, but there was an alternate modernism that venerated slowness.[15] I would argue that the college buildings of Lincoln Jones had a strange interior architectural space that slowed down both students and faculty, while at the same time privileging communalism over fragmentation and individualism. To walk through Jones' buildings was to be confronted with indecision and instability, a loss of sensory perception that made one see the world through different eyes. Their sense of the uncanny is what made entering them an aesthetic experience. Of course, today it would be seen as the height of madness for educational administrators to ask architects to design buildings that slowed down time and complicated perception.

Aside from Bagwell and me, the buildings had little value, intrinsic or pragmatic, for the administrators, faculty, architects, or the Steamboat Springs community. Of course I don't know this for sure. The architects for the Academic Center were paid $1,136,673 for their work.[16] The memo that Chad Novak, lead designer for H+L wrote about the Lincoln Jones buildings reveals that the hotel option was already on the table:

> We did have many conversations as a team, both H+L and CMC. In those discussions we verbally and through sketch looked at options of saving to demolishing the existing structures within the context of the new project. In the end the CMC Campus felt it was in the best interests for the future of the campus, programs, and development to move in the direction that ultimately took place.[17]

The uncanny nature of the Lincoln Jones buildings also kept the Steamboat Springs preservationist community silent. The local preservationist community is small and has limited power, enough to protect the Iron Spring from being touched but not enough to save the historically significant Harbor Hotel. They were silent when it came to the demolition of Willett Hall. Three important members of the preservationist community told me on separate occasions, for one, "I never liked the buildings in the first place;" for another, "Good riddance to bad rubbish;" and for a third, "That it is a good idea to get rid of them."

Arianthe Stettner wrote:

> I did all I could with the time/energy I had . . . We all have limited time and energy. Alas, I have been trying to save the historic 1900 collection house at the Museum, preventing the demolition of the Good Shepherd House cottage owned by the Catholic Church, and the loss of the little ice house by Casey's Pond. The past year has been a bad year for preservation in Steamboat."[18]

Meg Tully, director of Historic Routt County, told me that there was no discussion by that organization about saving Willett Hall.[19] The preservationist official at the City of Steamboat Springs was quite upset about its demolition, but because of the actions of the city council, the planning department was powerless to intervene on Woodchuck Hill.[20] At the last moment, the day of destruction, Colorado Preservation Inc.

Alpine Campus in 2012 before the Lincoln Jones buildings were demolished. Note that the two Lincoln Jones hexagonal buildings were still part of the campus. The completed Academic Center dominates the hillside. Photo by Cedar Beauregard, permission granted.

Demolition of Willett Hall. Photo by Ken Proper.

was finally prepared to list Willett Hall as a "Most Endangered Place." That was the classic "too little too late."[21] In the fall of 2012, with the help of two big trackhoes, Willett Hall was demolished.

When Willett Hall was demolished, a piece of history was destroyed and an aesthetically important building disappeared. Did something better remain? The empty space that once sheltered the Lincoln Jones buildings has not been used to build a hotel, but is now a parking lot. Lincoln Jones' Willett Hall was an expression of his architectural imagination and reflected the modernist ideals of the 1960s. Combined with Bristol Hall and the Academic Center it would have contributed to a visually stunning liberal arts campus.

Conclusion

THERE ARE TWO BASIC and different approaches to writing history. For some historians, history is a social science that uses statistics, mathematics, and rigorous methods to produce a description of "what actually happened" without any bias shown by the historian. For other historians, history is part of the humanities and a narrative that reflects the historian as much as it reflects the past. In this sense history is akin to literature, and I am a follower of this second approach. But unlike the novelist, who can make up any ending he or she imagines, as a narrative historian I am still constrained by the vectors of the past. Leo Tolstoy could have written that Anna Karenina boarded the train and moved into a pleasant life instead of throwing herself on the tracks. The narrative historian does not have that imaginative luxury.

It would be pleasant, and more pleasing to my readers, if I could end this book on a positive note. With a bit of the novelist's imagination I could write that the liberal arts and an exciting campus would again thrive on Woodchuck Hill. Steamboat Springs, after all, has always been a unique resort town with a high percentage of educated citizens, and today has a thriving literary, theater, and arts scene. Young people who come to college in Steamboat Springs are not typical of American students, and many of them enthusiastically elect to take liberal arts courses. Faculty members on the campus encourage internationalism. Suppose that the

121

innovative architectural design for a hotel were modified to create a living-learning center, where students lived and went to classes in the same building, as in the vision of Lincoln Jones. Suppose that the Steamboat Springs campus was truly "given its lead" by a district office in Glenwood Springs that valued the liberal arts and allowed the "Alpine Campus" to recruit more students and more full-time liberal arts faculty. I could then write the happy ending: that a campus could be designed on Woodchuck Hill to encourage the faculty and students to slow down, pay attention, and listen. Woodchuck Hill would then continue to work its uncanny magic on the Steamboat Springs Campus of Colorado Mountain College. Unfortunately, history is moving in a different direction.

It has been fifty years since higher education began on Woodchuck Hill. During this time the natural features of the hill have remained the same, with the same vegetation, underground springs, and energy lines. Educators and architects have attempted, and some have succeeded, to put their mark on the hill. Victor Hornbein's imaginative buildings and campus plans of 1964 failed to materialize. Robert Pietrowski's and Lincoln Jones' buildings of 1966 did materialize, and dominated the hill until the 1990s. John Vickery and Paul Hack then joined forces to make Bristol Hall a reality in 1993. Later in the 1990s a rather pedestrian dormitory was plunked down on the hill, and along with cheap metal buildings for maintenance. In 2010 an entrance to the campus from Lincoln Avenue was proposed and abandoned, and George Bagwell's campus plan ignored. In 2012 a new Academic Center that dominated the hill was constructed and the Lincoln Jones buildings torn down. In 2013 a hotel was proposed for the hill, but never built. As I write the conclusion, a greenhouse below the Academic Center has been approved, and there are future plans for an apartment building.

In Chapter One I quoted the American historian, Daniel J. Boorstin, who viewed American history in terms of a tension between the polarities of human beings as thinkers and human beings as makers. I transformed this idea of tension and polarity into a higher education that emphasized the liberal arts in contrast to higher education as vocational. Initially, higher education on Woodchuck Hill favored the "thinker" side, characterized by the liberal arts. This liberal arts vision of higher education motivated Lucy Bogue to found Yampa Valley College in the early 1960s. Robert Pietrowski and the educators of Colorado Alpine College in the middle 1960s continued the liberal arts tradition. The buildings that Lincoln Jones designed in the 1960s were inspired by that tradition. United States International University on Woodchuck Hill from the late 1960s until the early 1970s was a strange mixture of the liberal arts and financial chicanery.

When Colorado Mountain College—like most community colleges an institution that emphasized vocational education—took ownership of Woodchuck Hill, tension between vocational education and the liberal arts became manifest. The administrators and faculty at the Alpine Campus fought to keep the liberal arts vision alive on Woodchuck Hill as a unique entity within Colorado Mountain College. For twenty years, from 1980 to 2000, liberal arts courses were the "cadillac" on the hill, while vocational courses in ski business and resort management remained strong. In the 1990s Bristol Hall was conceived as an architectural home for the liberal arts. For several decades a high-quality, low-cost, open-admission liberal arts education for freshmen and sophomores flourished in Steamboat Springs.

After the turn of the twenty-first century, the emphasis on Woodchuck Hill slowly changed from liberal arts to vocational. Construction of the Academic Center, somewhat misnamed, symbolized this shift; it is a massive building that celebrates recreation, food preparation, and the market economy, part of a renamed "Steamboat Springs Campus," well integrated into Colorado Mountain College.[1] Like the other campuses of CMC, the Steamboat Springs Campus now emphasizes vocational programs—culinary arts, resort management, ski business, business, and sustainability.

The destruction of Lincoln Jones' buildings occurred because administrators wanted an upscale hotel connected to the Academic Center in order to increase the standing of the resort management and culinary programs.

123

If the introduction of four-year degrees by Colorado Mountain College, in sustainability and business at the present writing, has the same effect as at other four-year institutions, it will move the faculty further away from the unglamorous job of teaching freshmen and sophomores. New budget guidelines from the district office in 2014 severely penalized liberal arts courses, now mostly taught by low-paid adjuncts or online.[2] Spanish is the only foreign language taught. Many students, in their hurry to be vocational and in order to save money, now take "advanced placement" courses at their high schools, courses that may or may not transmit some knowledge and are a poor substitute for a genuine liberal arts education on a college campus.

One underlying theme of this book is that the critical thinking necessary for real education is not a continuous process, but a discontinuous one that advances through stages.[3] Both my own life history and my teaching experiences have convinced me that the higher stages of critical thinking develop during the ages of eighteen to twenty-one, that is, the time when young people are freshmen and sophomores in college.[4] This critical thinking requires a liberal arts education in an appropriate campus atmosphere. To fully explain this would require another book, but I would argue that if you push a young person too fast, or if a young person misses this stage of development because he or she is pragmatically oriented or pushed in a pragmatic direction, that person will later on experience a lack that will either require a return, with much more difficulty, to that earlier stage or will produce strange adult behavior.[5]

A second underlying theme of this book is that the United States was founded on the ideal that citizens of a democracy could attain a nonaristocratic version of the noble life through liberal arts education and that this education, peculiarly American, was closely tied to the Protestant idea of an authentic "calling." It entailed a vision of freedom and critical thinking that came from the European Enlightenment of the eighteenth century.

In the early 1950s the Harvard historian Crane Brinton published an influential book called *Ideas and Men*; the second half was published separately as *The Shaping of the Modern Mind*. In his conclusion to this book Brinton summarized the three basic principles of Western European thought: first, that there is an organization of the universe, "not evident to unreflective men, not provable by scientific methods, never wholly plain to the best and wisest of men, but an organization, not a chaos." The second principle was "the dignity of man." The third was the ideal of the flourishing life that came from the aristocratic culture of Greece and the Aristotelian ideal of the Golden Mean. Brinton contrasted this ideal with the ascetic Christian life and the modern manic (Faustian) approach to life. He then presented as the most acute of modern problems the ability of education to bring this aristocratic code of conduct to a mass democratic society: "The basic belief of eighteenth-century philosophers . . . was that the common man can lead this form of the good life now that the material basis lacking to the Greek masses is potentially available to all."[6] Brinton's vision required students to take a "time out" from their vocational concerns, emulate for a short period of time the contempt that aristocrats felt for economic grasping, and feel comfortable that the market economy would later offer a suitable vocational track. That economic reality was true in the 1950s. Now, almost seventy years later, it is clear that the market economy has changed.

The Eurocentric aristocratic path has lost its audience in the diverse culture of America because students, faculty, and administrators are subject to the manic behavior of an increasing aggressive and volatile marketplace. A large majority of today's students understand that they will have to adjust to marketplace values.[7] "They're willing to have a major they're not really interested in if they think there will be job growth in that field. They're much less likely than their predecessors to say they're in college to develop their personal values, or learn to get along with different people."[8] If you were to tell them to slow down and try to find authenticity, they would tell you that there isn't time for an authentic life, that the competition for jobs in America demands constant activity.[9] Now, in America, at all levels of higher education, from Harvard and Stanford through state universities and down to community colleges, institutions boast of their "practicality."[10] All politicians, both Republicans and Democrats, now demand practical education; recent proposals that colleges be rated according to how much money their graduates make will further cripple the liberal arts.[11] If higher education, particularly for freshmen and sophomores, is reduced to the efficient production of worker bees in buildings that resemble corporate headquarters, without pleasant natural surroundings, the vision of our founding fathers that democracy will produce noble citizens capable of critical thinking will be irrevocably lost.

Liberal arts education will continue to exist on Woodchuck Hill, nourished by a devoted faculty. However, in our speedy digital age it will be relegated to the edge of higher educational life on the hill. For those of us who have been part of the long liberal arts tradition on Woodchuck Hill, the end of that history is a sad and perhaps tragic conclusion, but eventually the students and faculty will adjust—some more easily than others—to the vocational demands of a capitalist world where economic incentives crowd out every other manner of being.[12] For the vast majority of American college students (except perhaps for those fortunate students in a few small and very expensive liberal arts colleges) a liberal arts education will be a lost reality, as much a fiction as *Anna Karenina*.

Appendix 1

Recent Books and Articles on Liberal Arts Education

Arum, Richard and Josipa Rokas. *Academically Adrift: Limited Learning on College Campuses.* Chicago: University of Chicago Press, 2011.

Brewer, Talbot. "The Coup That Failed: How the Near-Sacking of a University President Exposed the Fault Lines of American Higher Education," *Hedgehog Review,* Vol. 16, No. 2 (Summer 2014).

Brooks, David. "Becoming a Real Person," *New York Times,* September 11, 2014.

Delbanco, Andrew. *College: What It Was, and Should Be.* Princeton, New Jersey: Princeton University Press, 2012.

Deresiewicz, William. *Excellent Sheep: The Miseducation of the American Elite and the Way to a Meaningful Life.* New York: Free Press, 2014.

Edmundson, Mark. *Teacher: The One Who Made the Difference.* New York: Vintage Reprint, 2003.

Edmundson, Mark. *Why Teach?: In Defense of a Real Education.* New York: Bloomsbury Reprint, 2014.

Ferrall, Victor E., Jr. *Liberal Arts at the Brink.* Cambridge, Massachusetts: Harvard University Press, 2011.

Ginsberg, Benjamin. *The Fall of the Faculty: The Rise of the All-Administrative University and Why It Matters.* New York: Oxford, 2011.

Harpham, Geoffrey. *The Humanities and the Dream of America*. Chicago: University of Chicago Press, 2011.

Keeling, Ricard and Richard Hersh. *We're Losing Our Minds: Rethinking American Higher Education*. New York: St. Martin's Press, 2011.

Knonman, Anthony. *Education's End: Why Our Colleges and Universities Have Given Up on the Meaning of Life*. New Haven, Connecticut: Yale University Press, 2007.

Levine, Arthur. "Q & A With Arthur Levine," *New York Times Education Life Magazine*, November 4, 2012.

Lewin, Tamar. "As Interest Fades in the Humanities, Colleges Worry," *New York Times*, October 31, 2013.

Palmer, Parker and Arthur Zajonc. *The Heart of Higher Education*. San Francisco: Wiley, 2010.

Roche, Mark. *Why Choose The Liberal Arts*. Notre Dame, Indiana: University of Notre Dame Press, 2010.

Ross, Alex. "The Naysayers," *The New Yorker*, September 15, 2014

Schuessler, Jennifer. "Humanities Committee Sounds an Alarm," *New York Times*, June 18, 2013.

Appendix 2

The Architectural Career of Lincoln Jones after 1966

LINCOLN JONES WORKED as an architect in Steamboat Springs from 1966 to 1983. In the 1970s he divorced his wife, remarried, and acquired a stepson. He also opened a second office in Glenwood Springs, during a building boom there, and designed schools for Rifle and the Roaring Fork Valley. He had a friend with an airplane at the Steamboat Springs airport and flew between his two offices.[1]

Jones was an acerbic critic of urban sprawl and of sprawl in Steamboat Springs. In the early 1980s he taught planning courses at Colorado Mountain College and preached the benefits of compactness. He became a vociferous opponent of the extension of Steamboat Springs past its downtown area. He and Bob McHugh would drive Lincoln Avenue and imagine redesigning the buildings so that there was one theme. One of his predilections was for shingled half-mansard flat roofs, considered in the 1960s and 1970s a cheap and easy way to redesign a building. There was a joke in Steamboat Springs that Lincoln Jones wanted " . . . to give the town a case of the shingles."[2] In this he was not alone: Denver architect Marvin Knedler, who was also interested in the redesign of mountain towns, came to Steamboat Springs and designed mansard roofs for the

Lincoln Jones' half-mansard roof remodel of the Rabbit Ears Motel. Photo by Ken Proper.

Lincoln Jones' half-mansard roof on the Steamboat Springs Health and Recreation building. Photo by Ken Proper.

Marvin Knedler's mansard roof on the Routt County Bank building at 2nd Street and Lincoln Avenue. Knedler preferred full mansard roofs. Photo by Ken Proper.

Routt County Bank and for the building at the corner of 8th Street and Lincoln Avenue.[3]

Pat Carney, the present director of Steamboat Springs Health and Recreation, remembers Lincoln Jones and his mansard roofs well: "We haven't had that much of a problem with the flat roof—the mansards shed snow on people." Then Carney added:

> He was a great guy who was always very good to me. He recommended me for this job in 1975 and along with Dorothy Wither talked the rest of the board into hiring someone as young and inexperienced as I was. He was a great support to me until he left in November of 1983.[4]

In 1972 he remodeled the Leckenby House on Pahwintah Street. His design contains motifs that he had used in his design of the ski hill condominiums: sloping, irregular rooflines that give the house a sense of tension and movement.[5]

131

Leckenby House, Pahwintah Street, built in 1959. Lincoln Jones designed the home's 1972 addition. Photo by Ken Proper.

In 1970 Jones designed his own house on Fish Creek Falls Road, a dynamic circular structure set on a large corner lot and designed to fit into the contours of the land.[6] Jones was experimenting with new forms of space, and although one cannot find a direct link, the house is reminiscent of the sketches that Italian architect Paolo Soleri made in the 1960s .

In 1971 Jones designed a house for Robert W. Ralston, the owner of the Texaco station, on Pahwintah Street. Jones here showed his debt to Frank Lloyd Wright, with a cantilevered roof, a brick chimney vertically transecting the house, and the strong, horizontal lines of the balcony.

In 1971 Jones decided to build his own office on Pine Grove Road, and he borrowed directly from the ideas of Buckminster Fuller and designed his own geodesic domes. Jones and a crew of his friends built the domes themselves in the winter of 1971-1972.[7]

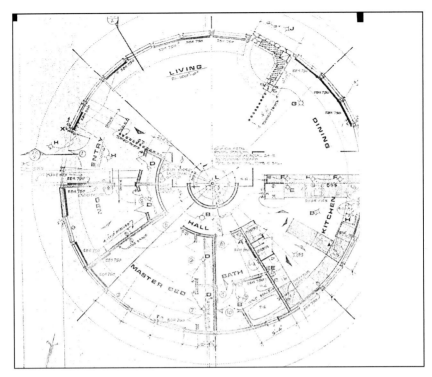

Lincoln Jones' plans for his Circular House on Fish Creek Falls Road, 1970. Courtesy of Robert S. Ralston. Permission by Glen Jones.

Views of Lincoln Jones' Circular House. Permission by Glen Jones. Photos by Ken Proper.

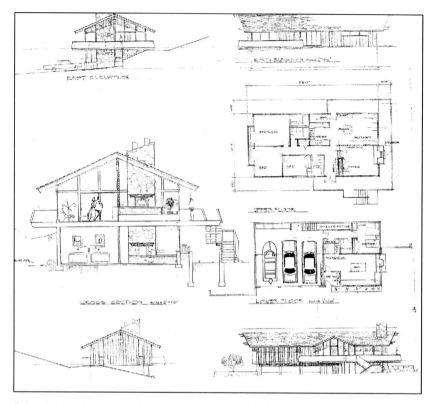

Robert W. Ralston House plans. Courtesy of Robert S. Ralston.

View of Robert W. Ralston House. Photo by Ken Proper.

134

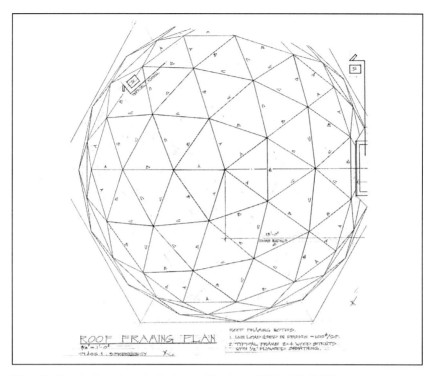

Plans for Lincoln Jones' geodesic domes. Courtesy of Robert S. Ralston.

Geodesic dome being built by Lincoln Jones. Permission by Catherine Lykken. Photo by Gary Lykken.

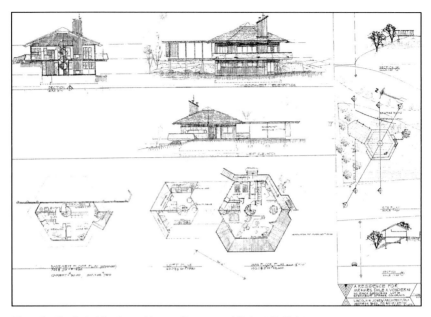

Plans for the Dale Vonderau House. Courtesy of Robert S. Ralston.

Vonderau House. Photo by Ken Proper.

Holloran House. Courtesy of Michael Holloran.

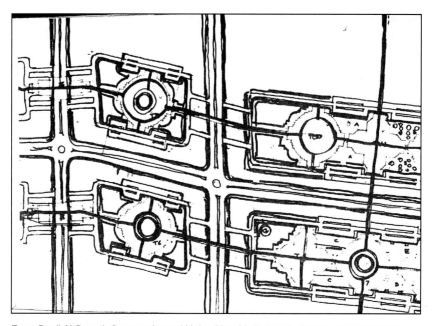

From Basil Al-Bayati, Community and Unity (New York: 1983). Courtesy of Glen Jones.

In 1972 Jones designed a house for Dale Vonderau in the Tree Haus subdivision. He used the same motifs that he had used in the ski area master plan of 1964, again reminiscent of Paolo Soleri's sketches and of Frank Lloyd Wright's use of thirty-degree angles. As usual, Jones obsessed over every detail of the work. Robert S. Ralston remembers him being dissatisfied with the railing on the deck, which did not satisfy his need for a strong, horizontal line.

After 1972, Lincoln Jones continued to work in Steamboat Springs and the Western Slope—schools, houses, churches, additions, and remodels—but the outlets for his really creative work increasingly diminished. Steamboat Springs was changing from the easy-going town of the 1960s to the increasingly regulated resort town of the 1970s. No longer could one build a circular house without a permit or build one's own geodesic dome. Commissions and regulations were now in place.

Lincoln Jones' final buildings in Steamboat Springs may be viewed as his retreat into the conformity to prevailing trends. They do not reflect his earlier aesthetic passions. In 1977 he designed a house for lawyer Michael Holloran on Colorado Highway 131. It is a very nice house, but there is little of the modernist Lincoln Jones in it.

By the 1980s modernism in architecture, whether of the more abstract or more organic varieties, had finally run its course. Adolf Loos wrote the first modernist architectural manifesto in 1908 and the work of Mies van der Rohe and Frank Lloyd Wright now seemed old-fashioned. Lincoln Jones' foundational point was modernist architecture, and it died in America in the 1970s. The important question for Jones was— what does one do in the aftermath?

Lincoln Jones left Steamboat Springs in 1983. He went to work as an architectural consultant for Trans-Gulf International, a multi-national oil company based in Qatar, on the Persian Gulf. Qatar is a Muslim country, and architecture is part of its religious heritage. However, if one is not a Muslim and simply looks at the architecture as architecture, it bears a strong resemblance to the austerity, lines, and angles of American modernist architecture. Then Lincoln Jones was offered a position on the staff of Qatar's ruler. He was " . . . allowed the full freedom of design which

Painting by Lincoln Jones.
Courtesy of Glen Jones.

was his trademark."[8] He told his son that Qatar was an "architect's dream" with big projects and lots of money.[9] Since Qatar had an authoritarian ruler, there were no planning commissions or regulations. We do not know exactly what Jones designed in Qatar, but he did give his son a book of architectural drawings on which he had collaborated. They show a clear linkage to his earliest work in Steamboat Springs: the master plan for the new ski area in 1964. We know that in Qatar, Jones lived with his wife and stepson, raced the Sheik's fleet of Ferrari's across the desert,[10] and became an expert and enthusiastic scuba diver. His life was far from Steamboat Springs, Colorado, but intellectually and artistically his life narrative was consistent and meaningful.

In 1988, while scuba diving in the Persian Gulf, Lincoln Jones had a heart attack and died. Because of Muslim law he was buried the next day in Qatar, now in a place unknown. An accomplished artist, Jones drew this picture of a minaret while in Qatar. Perhaps his grave is within the sound of the *salah*.

Lincoln Jones left a strong legacy in Steamboat Springs. Young architects who worked under him, Bob McHugh (now in Paonia, Colorado), Robert S. Ralston, and Joe Robbins, have all had distinguished architectural careers. Five of Lincoln Jones' buildings in Steamboat Springs were visionary and notable.[11] Two that were commercial structures have disappeared: his geodesic domes and the real-estate building at the corner of Pine Grove Road and U.S. Highway 40 (now a Walgreens store).[12] Two are houses: his Circular House and the Robert W. Ralston House. The fifth was his most unique and imaginative design, the buildings for Yampa Valley College in 1966—now demolished.

Abbreviations for Sources Used in Endnotes

CMC Archives: Colorado Mountain College, Steamboat Springs Campus Archives, Steamboat Springs, Colorado.

Hornbein Papers, DPL: Victor Hornbein Papers, Western History Collection, Denver Public Library, Denver, Colorado.

OAHP: Office of Archaeology and Historic Preservation, History Colorado (formerly Colorado Historical Society), Denver, Colorado.

Routt County Clerk: Routt County, Colorado, Clerk and Recorder's Office Records, Steamboat Springs, Colorado.

Steamboat Springs Clerk: City Clerk's Office Records, City of Steamboat Springs, Colorado.

Steamboat Springs Planning: Planning Commission Records, City of Steamboat Springs, Colorado.

Steamboat Springs School: RE-2 School District Archives, Steamboat Springs, Colorado

Tread Museum: Tread of Pioneers Museum Archives, Steamboat Springs, Colorado.

Endnotes

Introduction

1 See David Brooks, "Becoming a Real Person," *New York Times*, Opinion Section, September 11, 2014.

2 Talbot Brewer, "The Coup That Failed: How the Near-Sacking of a University President Exposed the Fault Lines of American Higher Education," *Hedgehog Review*, Vol. 16, No. 2 (Summer, 2014), p. 82.

3 Brewer, *Hedgehog Review*, Vol. 16, No. 2. The decline of liberal arts education has recently spawned a large number of books and articles. See list of recent books and articles about liberal arts education in Appendix 1.

4 Tamar Lewin, "As Interest Fades in the Humanities, Colleges Worry," *New York Times*, October 31, 2013.

5 Friedrich Nietzsche, *Beyond Good and Evil* (1886; New York: Oxford University Press, 1998), p. 169.

Chapter One: American Liberal Arts Education

1 Daniel J. Boorstin, *The Lost World of Thomas Jefferson* (Chicago: University of Chicago Press, 1948, 1993), p. 4.

2 Boorstin, *Lost World*, p. 218.

3 See "Liberal Arts Education," Wikipedia. In Latin, *liberal* means "worthy of a free person."

4 Anthony Knonman, *Education's End: Why Our Colleges and Universities Have Given Up on the Meaning of Life* (New Haven, Connecticut: Yale University Press, 2007), p. 35.

5 Richard Sennett, *The Craftsman* (New Haven, Connecticut: Yale University Press, 2008), p. 58.

6 Quoted in Josef Pieper, Leisure: *The Basis of Culture* (New York: New American Library, 1952, 1963), p. 38.

7 Victor E. Ferrall, Jr., *Liberal Arts at the Brink* (Cambridge, Massachusetts: Harvard University Press), p. 46.

8 Andrew Delbanco, *College: What It Was, Is, and Should Be* (Princeton, New Jersey: Princeton University Press, 2012), pp. 3, 46. See also, Laurence Steinberg, "The Case for Delayed Adulthood," *New York Times*, September 21, 2014.

9 Jonathan Coulson, Paul Roberts, and Isabelle Taylor, *University Planning and Architecture: The Search for Perfection* (New York: Routledge, 2011), p. vi.

10 See website: "Thomas Jefferson: The Architect of a Nation."

11 See "Thomas Jefferson," website.

12 Joshua Pollard and Andrew Reynolds, *Avebury: The Biography of a Landscape* (Stroud, Gloucestershire, Great Britain: The History Press, 2002), p. 47.

13 Carl Becker, *The Heavenly City of the Eighteenth Century Philosophers* (2nd ed.; New Haven, Connecticut: Yale University Press, 2003).

14 The critics of both the classical Greeks and of Jefferson point out that these visions rested on the institution of slavery and economic exploitation, and that this is a serious objection to their ideals. However, it is possible to theorize about a flourishing life without exploitation and to honor Jefferson despite his many faults. See, for example, the recent book by Jon Meacham, *Thomas Jefferson and the Art of Power* (New York: Random House, 2013).

15 Coulson et al., *University Planning*, p. 13.

16 Harold Hellenbrand, *The Unfinished Revolution: Education and the Politics of Thomas Jefferson* (Newark, Delaware: University of Delaware Press, 1990), p. 159.

17 Boorstin, *Lost World*, p. 49. The idea of the chain of being, now anachronistic, survived until the 1950s. See Joseph Wood Krutch, *The Great Chain of Life* (Boston: Houghton Mifflin, 1956).

18 For this debate, see Jacques Barzun, *The House of the Intellect* (New York: Harper, 1959), p. 96n.

19 The terms are from Pieper, *Leisure*, p. 21.

Chapter Two: An Apprenticeship in Liberal Arts Education

1 It was built in 1914 and designed by Arthur Hussander, born in 1885, who was appointed architect for the Chicago Public Schools in 1910 and designed square buildings with classical facades all over Chicago. See Chicago Historic Schools website.

2 The building was modernized and made more internally friendly in 1966 and is now called Hyde Park Academy.

3 In the 1950s rebels and nonconformists bought shirts with bent collars like the singer Billy Eckstine, wore pants with pegged or tight cuffs, and cut their hair with a part in the back called a DA, or "duck's ass," like Elvis Presley.

4 I later found out that it was designed by Frederick Law Olmsted.

5 The University of Chicago was founded by John D. Rockefeller, who endowed it with an English Gothic style of architecture.

6 Lance Factor, *Chapel in the Sky* (DeKalb, Illinois: Northern Illinois University Press, 2010), pp. 48-49.

7 Lance Factor, a professor at Knox College, made these connections long after I had graduated. See *Chapel in the Sky.*

8 Leland Stanford founded Leland Stanford Junior University after the death of his son and named the university after his son.

9 Stanford Historical Society, *Sandstone and Tile*, Vol. 11, No. 2-3 (Winter-Spring 1987), pp. 6-7.

10 Richard Sennett recently wrote, "All skills, even the most abstract, begin as bodily practices." See *The Craftsman*, p. 10.

11 See Jon Margolis, *The Last Innocent Year: America in 1964—The Beginning of the 1960's* (New York: Morrow, 1999), and James T. Patterson, *The Eve of Destruction: How 1965 Transformed America* (New York: Basic Books, 2012).

12 Robert A. Heinlein's 1961 book, *Stranger in a Strange Land*, had an important effect on youth in the 1960s.

13 Of course this was an outrageous and unfair comparison that I actually articulated during a speech at an anti-war demonstration in front of the CSU student center in 1969. It was my tongue-in-cheek way of trying to *épater le bourgeois*, and it did indeed upset the old guard of the history department. However, historians have accepted the fact that both fascist and communist architecture were remarkably similar. See Tony Judt, *Thinking the Twentieth Century* (New York: Penguin Press, 2012), p. 165. To its credit, CSU later tried to modify the

most horrendous aspects of this architecture, beginning with an imaginative remodel of the library and a modification of the student center. Replacement of the football stadium is in the planning stages.

14 "Fear and loathing" was the trademark phrase of the writer Hunter Thompson, popular in the 1960s. See *Fear and Loathing at Rolling Stone: The Essential Writing of Hunter S. Thompson* (New York: Simon and Schuster, 2012).

15 History was considered a social science at CSU because, as far as I could tell, in the pecking order of the university the social sciences received a bit more money than the humanities. The slogan was, "If there is a 'Science' on the door, there is a rug on the floor," a reference to the fact that the humanities building had concrete floors while the social science building had carpets.

16 Robert M. Pirsig, *Zen and the Art of Motorcycle Maintenance* (New York: Bantam Books, 1974, 1981), pp. 128-130.

17 Dylan Trigg, *The Memory of Place: A Phenomenology of the Uncanny* (Athens, Ohio: Ohio University Press, 2012), p. 26.

18 George Elton Mayo, *The Human Problems of an Industrial Civilization* (New York: Routledge Reprint, 2003).

19 See Adam Hochschild, "Berkeley: What We Didn't Know," *The New York Review of Books*, May 23, 2013, pp. 35-37.

20 I met Kerensky at Stanford and discussed his failure with him.

21 For an insightful view of how difficult it was to adjust to the changing atmosphere after 1968, see Liel Leibovitz, *A Broken Hallelujah: Rock and Roll, Redemption and the Life of Leonard Cohen* (New York: W.W. Norton, 2014).

22 See James E. Hansen II, ed., *Harry Rosenberg, An Oral History Interview and Papers with Commentary by Those Who Knew Him* (Fort Collins, Colorado: Colorado State University, Communications and Creative Services, 2011).

23 Wayman, a Canadian, has since become one of the most famous poets in Canada.

24 For a similar sentiment, see Elize Hittmann, "It Felt Like Love," *New Yorker*, November 18, 2013, p. 17.

Chapter Three: Yampa Valley College

1 See OAHP website: "Architects of Colorado: Victor Hornbein." Hornbein would go on to design the Denver Botanic Gardens, and in his lifetime he designed some thirty-six houses and eighty public buildings.

2 See OAHP website.

3 Population in Routt County, Colorado, declined from 10,512 in 1940 to 8,940 in 1950 to 5,900 in 1960. See State Demography Office, Colorado Division of Local Government website: "Population Statistics."

4 Bonnie Bogue, "Welcome from Lucy Bogue." Typescript of 2011 speech Bonnie Bogue gave in Steamboat Springs. CMC Archives.

5 Willa Kane, "Frontier Diary," *Garfield Post Independent* (Glenwood Springs, Colorado), April 5, 2011.

6 Lucy Bogue, "Presentation Sheets." CMC Archives. Some sheets are reproduced in Lucy Bogue, *Miracle on a Mountain* (San Francisco: Strawberry Hill Press, 1997), pp. 87-89.

7 Charlotte Perry file. Tread Museum.

8 Reinhold Niebuhr, *Faith and History* (New York: Scribners, 1949).

9 The European view after World War II was more cynical: the Enlightenment was seen as having produced a fatal dialectic that led to wars and totalitarianism. See Max Horkeimer and Theodor W. Adorno, *Dialectic of Enlightenment* (German edition 1944; English translation 1947; republished by Verso Books, 1996).

10 "Krista Tippett interview with Alice Rivlin, October 28, 2012." From National Public Radio program, *On Being*.

11 Bogue, *Miracle*, p. 12. In a letter to the author dated September 4, 2011, former Yampa Valley College instructor George Tolles wrote, "I would guess the greatest influence was Lucy Bogue's association with Perry-Mansfield and its founders."

12 "Yampa Valley College First Series Debenture" brochure. Hornbein Papers, DPL.

13 Bogue, *Miracle*, p. 2.

14 "Letter from Lucy Bogue to Storm Mountain People, January 1962." Hornbein Papers, DPL.

15 See Stefan Muthesius, *The Postwar University: Utopianist Campus and College* (New Haven, Connecticut: Yale University Press, 2000), p. 14.

16 "Yampa Valley College 1964 brochure." CMC Archives, and Hornbein Papers, DPL. The teachers were an exceptional group, mostly recruited from Strawberry Park. Bob Shaw was a local Steamboat Springs' boy who had gone to the University of Colorado for a degree in philosophy. Gene Cook was recruited from the Whiteman School, where he later became headmaster. Later in the 1960s he also founded a private school, Buckingham Academy, on Rabbit Ears Pass. Chris Fetcher taught music. Jerry Randolph, a teacher in Denver attracted by the mountains, taught history. Elizabeth St. Louis, the daughter of an Italian diplomat and educated in Italy, taught French, Latin, Italian, and art history. Bob Krear, who retired from the U.S. Forest Service and held a doctorate, taught science. Pat Whitlow, with a master's degree in philosophy, taught literature and humanities. Elwin Powell taught math. The pay was minimal: George Tolles remembers receiving less than $3,000 a year in 1964. Tolles supplemented his income in the summer by teaching at a naval reserve college.

17 Bonnie Bogue 2011 speech typescript. CMC Archives; "Personal interview with George Tolles, October 19, 2012."

18 Lucy and Arthur Bogue were good friends with Farrington "Ferry" Carpenter, a graduate of Princeton University and Harvard Law School who became a lawyer in Hayden. Carpenter initially raised $30,000 for the new college. Carpenter does not mention Lucy Bogue or the college in his autobiography. See Farrington R. Carpenter, *Confessions of a Maverick: An Autobiography* (Denver: State Historical Society of Colorado, 1984).

19 Everett "Ev" Bristol, chairman of the board, was born on a farm near Ansley, Nebraska, in 1923. When the dust bowl forced the family off the farm, the Bristols moved to Steamboat Springs in 1935. In 1940 he graduated from the University of Colorado with a degree in engineering and served in the U.S. Navy in World War II. In 1947 he joined Colorado Utilities as an engineer, and when that turned into the Yampa Valley Electric Association (YVEA), he worked there until his death. George Sauer, born in 1911, was raised on a ranch near Hugo, Colorado, started teaching at age 19, put himself through Colorado State College (later Colorado College of Education and then University of Northern Colorado), taught in Nebraska, started teaching in Steamboat Springs in 1944, and in 1949 became superintendent of the Steamboat Springs school system. Jim Golden, another influential board member, was director of YVEA. Marv Crawford, born in 1932 in Steamboat Springs, competed in the 1956 Olympics and in the 1960s established Ski Country Enterprises, a real-estate firm. Norbert Eugene "Del" Haute was a Denver auto mechanic who fixed a car for a watch salesman who then talked Haute into starting a jewelry business in Steamboat Springs in 1946. Charles Leckenby was editor and publisher of the *Steamboat Pilot*. Don Kinney was born in Helena, Montana, in 1929, came to Hahns Peak in 1932 to live with his aunt and uncle, got a degree in pharmacy from the University of Colorado in1951, and became the owner of two drug stores in Steamboat Springs. He was a ski jumper and promoted the sport. Information compiled from Tread Museum files.

20 "Interview with John Fetcher," Steamboat Springs High School newspaper, *Three Wire Winter* (Steamboat Springs, Colorado), 1985. Tread Museum.

21 "Personal interview with Frankie Stetson of Oak Creek, December 2010."

22 "*Three Wire Winter* Fetcher interview." Tread Museum.

23 "*Three Wire Winter* Fetcher interview." Tread Museum.

24 Fetcher sold part of his own ranchland for Steamboat Lake, and he sold land around the new ski area to make payroll. He later admitted that in his haste to sell land, the ski area became hemmed in by early subdivisions. "*Three Wire Winter* Fetcher interview." Tread Museum.

25 When the ski area did not make as much economic headway as Fetcher had hoped because in the early 1960s it was still difficult to get large numbers of skiers to Steamboat Springs, he sold the area to the Ling-Temco-Vought (LTV) Aerospace Corporation. Fetcher later said that Jim Temple "gave up" on the ski area because of financial difficulties and "another group from Denver took over." "*Three Wire Winter* Fetcher interview." Tread Museum. Fetcher had a rival for the lease on the government land around the ski area: Tom Hinsdale, who owned the "Cave Inn" bar and bowling alley and 550 acres at the road going into the ski area. Hinsdale had also planned a ski area and hired Boulder architect Carl Worthington to design the buildings. When Fetcher sold to LTV, Hinsdale also sold his land. It is now a shopping center.

26 In 1990 Stephens College decided to sell the camp. The "Friends of Perry-Mansfield" raised $1.1 million to keep it running, and the camp remains an important part of Steamboat Springs' culture.

27 "Personal interview with John Whittum, December 2010."

28 Various projections are found in the CMC Archives and Hornbein Papers, DPL.

29 This idea was not unique to Fetcher; selling land to support education was embedded in a long American tradition. See Daniel J. Boorstin, *The Americans: The Democratic Experience* (New York: Vintage, 1974), p. 277.

30 "Minutes, Board of Trustees, Town of Steamboat Springs, Colorado, August 30, 1962." Steamboat Springs Clerk.

31 Bogue, *Miracle*, p. 39.

32 Bogue, *Miracle*, p. 59.

33 Newell P. Campbell, *Geology Profiles of the Steamboat Springs Area* (Steamboat Springs, Colorado: self-published, 2004), p. 53.

34 For the history of Woodchuck Ditch, see "The Woodchuck Ditch: Statement of Significance," an attachment to Resolution No. 05-087, Routt County Board of Commissioners, October 18, 2005. The early settlers from the East mistook the mountain marmot for a species of eastern woodchuck.

35 "Memo from Walsh Environmental Services, June 29, 2010." Steamboat Springs Planning.

36 "Minutes, Board of Trustees, Town of Steamboat Springs, Colorado, November 8, 1963." Steamboat Springs Clerk.

37 "Minutes, Board of Trustees, Town of Steamboat Springs, Colorado, November 15, 1963." Steamboat Springs Clerk.

38 Bogue, *Miracle*, p. 59.

39 Bogue, *Miracle*.

40 Hornbein Papers, DPL.

41 Hornbein Papers, DPL.

42 Book 7, Page 18; Book 196, Page 385; and Book 300, Page 583. Routt County Clerk. The two quarter sections (eighty acres) on Woodchuck Hill were originally bought by James Crawford from the Steamboat Springs Company in 1891. The land remained unused and in 1914, at the time of the first winter ski carnival in Steamboat Springs, Carl Howelsen erected a ski jump there. He soon learned that the winter sun directly hit the hill and moved his ski jump across the Yampa River to a north-facing slope. The lower forty-acre section was deeded back to the town of Steamboat Springs in 1941 for educational use, while the other quarter section remained in private hands. Several small parcels were carved out of the town's quarter section, and in 1961 the town sold 1.4 acres on U.S. Highway 40 to Jim Temple to start a drive-in restaurant. See also the map owned by Woodchuck Ditch Company.

43 Book 325, Page 329. Routt County Clerk.

44 Book 317, Page 328. Routt County Clerk.

45 "Yampa Valley College newsletter, 1964." CMC Archives.

46 These possibilities were again drawn by AndersonMasonDale Architects for a proposed building in 1990. Steamboat Springs Planning.

47 "Debenture." Hornbein Papers, DPL. To sell these debentures, Yampa Valley College sent out a brochure signed by Chairman of the Board of Directors Ev Bristol that asked for funds to begin a building program. The brochure included a projected budget for 1964-1965 that

reflected Hornbein's optimism: income from $32,412 in 1963-1964 jumped to $608,300 due to a projected $500,000 from the sale of the bonds. Tuition was to double, based on the projected arrival of new students, and room and board was to bring in $50,000 more.

48 A local Olympic ski hero, Buddy Werner, was killed in an avalanche while filming a commercial in Germany, and Storm Mountain was renamed for him.

49 Hornbein and Bogue were influenced by the example of Windham College in Putney, Vermont, where Bogue traveled in September 1964 (in *Miracle*, Bogue has the wrong date of 1965) for the inauguration of Eugene Winslow as president. Windham was founded as Vermont Institute in 1951, became Windham in 1954, but was accredited only in 1967. Even without accreditation Windham received $4.3 million from the federal government in 1964 for new buildings.

50 Chuck Leckenby, "Editorial," *Steamboat Pilot* (Steamboat Springs, Colorado), June 17, 1965.

51 Bogue, *Miracle*, pp. 107-108.

52 "Letter from Victor Hornbein to Lucy Bogue, March 11, 1965." Hornbein Papers, DPL.

Chapter Four: Lincoln Jones

1 Information about Lincoln Jones from "Personal interview with Robert S. Ralston, December 6, 2010"; "Personal interview with Joe Robbins, December 14, 2010"; and "Personal interview with Carl Worthington, December 16, 2010."

2 See David G. DeJong, Frank Gehry, and Bruce Goff, *Toward Absolute Architecture* (Cambridge, Massachusetts: Massachusetts Institute of Technology Press, 1988).

3 Alan Hess and Alan Weintraub, *Frank Lloyd Wright: Mid-Century Modern* (New York: Rizzoli, 2007), p. 14.

4 Alain de Botton, *The Architecture of Happiness* (New York: Pantheon, 2006), p. 63.

5 See Michael Paglia, Leonard Segel, and Diane Wray, "Historic Context of Modern Architecture in Boulder, Colorado, 1947-1977," City of Boulder Planning Department, 2000.

6 Fuller came to the World Affairs Conference in 1956, 1957, 1959-1961, 1965, 1967-1968. "Personal email from Melinda Painter of the Conference on World Affairs, January 4, 2011." See Buckminster Fuller, *Utopia or Oblivion: The Prospects for Humanity* (New York: Bantam Books, 1949).

7 Jones left no notes or diaries that would document his influences, but from Jones' drawings I would argue that the spiritual architect, Paolo Soleri (1919-2013), had a strong influence on Jones. See Paolo Soleri, *Matter Becoming Spirit: The Archology of Paolo Soleri* (New York: Anchor Books Doubleday, 1973).

8 Colleen M. O'Dwyer, "Architect Biography," *The Camera and Clipboard: Historical and Architectural Survey Newsletter of the Colorado Historical Society*, No. 16 (July, 2007), pp. 3-4.

9 For a biography of Tom Nixon, see Tom Nixon website. Nixon later had a distinguished career with the firm of Nixon, Brown, Brokaw, & Bowen in Boulder.

10 See 1949 photograph of the Henry Neils house, Minneapolis, Minnesota, in Hess and Weintrab, *Frank Lloyd Wright*, p. 315. See also photograph of Unitarian Meeting House, Shorehood Hills, Wisconsin, in Bruce Pfeiffer, ed., *The Essential Frank Lloyd Wright* (Princeton, New Jersey: Princeton University Press, 2010), p. 420.

11 Although the church now stands empty, it will be saved. A new, four-story building surrounds it on three sides.

12 From a March 1962 clipping about Lincoln Jones in the archives of the Boulder Historical Society. A symposium, "Concrete Utopias: 1960s Architecture and Urbanism," was held at the University of Houston in February 2011.

13 The Robert S. Ralston architectural office in Steamboat Springs still has most of the plans that Lincoln Jones executed; they number in the thousands.

14 "Personal telephone interview with Bob McHugh, December 7, 2010."

15 Dee Richards, "Notes for 'Nice People, Good Deeds,'" in *Steamboat Today* Archives, Steamboat Springs, Colorado.

16 Towny Anderson, "Eugene Sternberg's Socially Conscious Architectural Legacy in Colorado," *Colorado Preservationist: The Colorado Preservation Journal*, (Winter/Spring, 2010).

17 See "Interview with Tor Westgaard," Bud Werner Memorial Library Archives, Steamboat Springs, Colorado.

18 "Stetson interview."

19 Bogue, *Miracle*, p. 111.

20 "Personal communication from Karen Malcolm, Robert Pietrowski's daughter, July 23, 2010."

21 "Personal interview with George Tolles, December 5, 2010."

22 "Tolles 2010 interview."

23 *Yampa Valley College Newsletter*, Summer 1965. Hornbein Papers: DPL.

24 "Malcolm communication."

25 John Whittum remembers Pietrowski saying this when in 1966 he gave the commencement address at the Lowell Whiteman School. "Whittum interview."

26 *Yampa Valley College Newsletter*, Summer 1965. Hornbein Papers: DPL.

27 "Letter from Victor Hornbein to Lucy Bogue, October 7, 1964." Hornbein Papers: DPL.

28 "Letter from Victor Hornbein to Robert Pietrowski, September 15, 1965." Hornbein Papers: DPL.

29 When he quit, Hornbein refunded $995 of the $3,065 he claimed that the college owed him because he "believed in the mission of the college." "Letter from Victor Hornbein to Robert Pietrowski, November 4, 1965." Hornbein Papers: DPL.

30 For academic architecture in the 1960s, see Muthesius, *The Postwar University*, pp. 50-53, and Coulson et al., *University*, p. 29.

31 The first mention of this authority was an editorial by Charles Leckenby in the *Steamboat Pilot*, July 21, 1966.

32 "Minutes, Steamboat Springs school board, April 4, 1966." Steamboat Springs School. George Sauer was superintendent of schools and Ev Bristol was on the school board, and both were directors of YVC and Yampa College Building Authority.

33 "Minutes, Board of Trustees, Town of Steamboat Springs, June 10, 1966." Steamboat Springs Clerk. On that same date, the deed to Yampa Valley College was recorded in Routt County: Book 325, Page 329. Routt County Clerk. On July 1966, the Yampa Valley College Building Authority signed an agreement with the Central Bank of Denver for first mortgage bonds on land that it "will acquire" and mentioned the Steamboat Springs school district as a "future beneficiary: Book 325, Page 513. Routt County Clerk. On September 7, 1966, the authority legally transferred land from YVC to itself: Book 326, Page 506. Routt County Clerk. On September 13, 1966, the authority leased back the land to YVC: Book 326, Page 563. Routt County Clerk.

34 A list of bondholders is in the CMC Archives. Of the $900,000, Yampa Valley College director Ev Bristol was in for $2,000, Jim Golden for $1,000 and Don Kinney for $3,000. Charlotte Perry invested $2,000. John Fetcher did not invest. Most of the investors were within a 300-mile radius.

35 The bonds were to yield 5 percent interest and the lease between the college and the authority stated that the payment from the college to the authority would begin in 1966 at $58,512 and increase every year: $68,512 in 1969 and $79,200 in 1979, when the bonds would begin to be paid off, continuing until 1996 when they would be paid in full.

36 The consequences of limiting the bonds to a small tract created a legal and survey muddle that got more confusing over the years. The only legal document that ties the Steamboat Springs school district to the college land is a deed between the Yampa Valley College Building Authority and the school district on June 30, 1969, that gives the school district a "reversionary interest" in the small tract that the college buildings occupied. But the term "reversionary" is not defined in this document or other relevant documents, and is open to a wide range of interpretations. In 1907 Colorado law defined "reversionary" as " . . . the undisposed portion remaining in a grant when that grantor conveys less than his or her whole estate and therefore, retains a portion of the title." That the school district was to get the land after the bonds were redeemed was known at the time; Kirchner & Co. stated it in an ad placed in the *Steamboat*

Pilot on September 26, 1966. It was forgotten over time, and only remembered when Colorado Mountain College planned a new building in 2010 that encroached on the small tract.

37 One of the buildings did reach outside the limits imposed by the 1.45 acres. In 1967 the Yampa Valley College Building Authority bought an additional 0.61 acres from YVC to cover the area where the building exceeded the original 1.4 acres: Book 339, Page 518. Routt County Clerk.

38 "Personal interview with Glen Jones, Lincoln Jones' son, December 2010."

39 See photograph of Alfred and Matilda Wilson Hall, Michigan State University, East Lansing Michigan, designed by R. R. Calder and Associates in 1960; and in Muthesius, *Postwar University*, p. 36.

40 Anthony Vidler, *The Architectural Uncanny* (Cambridge, Massachusetts: Massachusetts Institute of Technology Press, 1992), p. 8.

41 James Joyce's final novel, *Finnigan's Wake*, demonstrates the uncanny in literature.

42 Vidler argues that structures do not themselves possess uncanny properties, but are uncanny because they act, historically or culturally, as representations of estrangement. See Vidler, *The Architectural Uncanny*, p. 12. But the Lincoln Jones buildings, in fact, did possess real uncanny properties.

43 This observation is based on an informal survey that I made of alumni who came back to the reunion of 2011. Every former student with whom I talked was positive about the buildings. This was in contrast to later opinion in Steamboat Springs, which was negative because the buildings were used for other purposes.

44 This was pointed out to me in an email from former Yampa Valley College student Ronni Connelly, who also thought that " . . . the buildings were ahead of their time."

45 On the difference between "feeling" and "being," see Katherine Withy, "Heidegger on Being Uncanny," doctoral dissertation, University of Chicago, 2009.

46 Jones here predated the ideas of Henri Lefebvre in "Toward an Architecture of Enjoyment" (1973) by almost a decade. See Henri Lefebvre, "Toward an Architecture of Enjoyment," *Artforum*, April 2014, pp. 232-237.

47 *Steamboat Pilot*, May 5, 1966.

48 This proved to be a mistake because the roofs leaked. Robert S. Ralston, a Steamboat Springs architect who later worked with Jones, claims that the basic idea was sound although the construction was not.

49 "Personal email from Bob McHugh, 2010." A local builder, Joe Bonny, was given the contract.

50 In addition to Woodchuck Hill, Monson had successfully urged the town to donate land for the hot springs pool. See the *Steamboat Pilot*, January 6, 1966.

51 The naming of Bogue Hall was ironic because Lucy Bogue hated the Lincoln Jones buildings.

52 *Steamboat Pilot*, September 29, 1966.

53 Joe Bonny actually poured concrete footers for the proposed administration building that were found when Bristol Hall was constructed in 1993.

54 *Steamboat Pilot*, November 24, 1966.

55 CMC Archives.

56 *Steamboat Pilot*, May 27, 1965.

57 Pietrowski had long been a friend of Curtis, and Curtis referred potential students to YVC. "Personal letter from Karen Malcolm, December 20, 2010."

58 David H. Roach, "One Night Stand," *The Talisman*, 1966 (Vol. 2, No. 1), p. 1. When Pietrowski left, Roach was also kicked out of the school. His name was not mentioned in the brochure for the 2011 reunion of students.

59 According to Willy Markowitz, a former YVC student, when the Hell's Angels rode through town in 1965, one director of the college suggested that the citizens arm themselves and shoot them. "Personal interview with Willy Markowitz, May 11, 2011."

60 *Hayden Valley Press*, May 5, 1966. The case was dismissed because Allen proved that he was trying to break up a fight between students and cowboys. Reprinted in *Yampa Valley Colorado Alpine College Reunion Book*, n.d., n.p. The evolution of ranch culture from the easy tolerance of the 1950s to the intolerance of 1960-1980 has, to my knowledge, never been studied. Antagonism in Routt County continued in the 1970s and culminated in 1972 when cowboys

kicked out the eye of a hippie in Oak Creek. Hostility diminished after the 1980s with the gradual growth of a tourist cowboy industry and ranches appropriated by wealthy Americans who only emulated cowboys. Today, all but a handful of ranches in Routt County are hobby ranches for wealthy Americans.

61 "Tolles 2010 interview."
62 Bogue, *Miracle*, p. 120.
63 *Miracle*, p. 120.
64 *Miracle*, p. 120.
65 "Whittum interview."
66 The money had been borrowed and the contracts had been signed for construction of the remaining buildings.

Chapter Five: Colorado Mountain College

1 First came Jim Godwin, an ex-military chemist and soil scientist. After Godwin had a heart attack and retired, he was replaced in the fall of 1967 by Dwight Corder, another ex-military science teacher. In the winter of 1967 Corder was replaced by Richard Roper, an ordained minister who had been academic dean at Ricker College in Maine, who, in turn, was replaced in the spring of 1968 by Ted Wahler, a businessman from Denver. Bogue, *Miracle*, pp. 121-123.
2 "That was my first taste of decisions being made at the top without input sought from the faculty," commented Lucy Bogue in her book, *Miracle*, p. 121.
3 Yampa Valley Electric Association, *Rocky Mountain Rural Life*, 1967. Tread Museum.
4 In *Yampa Valley Colorado Alpine College Reunion Book*, n.d., n.p.
5 See website for Kenya University, the only branch of Rust's educational empire still functioning.
6 Gilbert Johnson, "An Education in Real Estate: The USIU Land Rush," *The New Leader*, June 28, 1971, pp. 11-14. CMC Archives. With the land expansion, the student population of USIU only increased from 3,000 to 3,800 students.
7 For the change of title, see Book 337, Page 495. Routt County Clerk. Rust was not a real-estate salesman; he preferred to mortgage land and let someone else sell it. At the same time the directors of Colorado Alpine College transferred a road easement into the small tract to USIU. For the transfer of road easement, see Book 338, Page 536. Routt County Clerk.
8 "Personal email from Tom McCoy, January 24, 2011." McCoy had taught English under Richard Roper's presidency at Ricker College and joined two other Ricker teachers at Colorado Alpine College as the "Maine Mafia." After USIU took over, Rust told McCoy that he would have to change his syllabus and remove some film material. McCoy declined and left Steamboat Springs.
9 Johnson, "USIU Land Rush," *New Leader*.
10 See the David E. Fleming Company, "Engineering Inspection of Ski Lift Facilities at Woodchuck Hill Ski Area, Steamboat Springs, Colorado, January 1972, prepared for Colorado Alpine Campus, United States International University." CMC Archives.
11 "Personal interview with George Tolles, July 2011."
12 Book 354, Page 284. Routt County Clerk.
13 The Yampa Valley College Building Authority, having changed its name to the Steamboat Springs College Association, received a judgment in a Denver court against USIU, and the association was able to send pro-rated checks to its bondholders with a letter that the checks would not have value if USIU declared bankruptcy, which it did in 1978. "Letter from Ev Bristol to Doc Utterbeck, June 7, 1976." Tread Museum.
14 Denver District Court Action No. C-54854. I could not find any evidence that Rust was ever charged with a crime. The USIU continued on, but in 1990 Rust was stripped of all governing power.
15 "Richard's notes." *Steamboat Today* Archives.
16 John Grassby, attorney for Steam Realty, said that Citibank would indeed send teams of men to Steamboat Springs—he called them "the suit people"—but each time it would be different

men, and he would spend several days bringing them up to speed. "Personal interview with John Grassby, November 2012." On the Steam Realty and David Combs dealings, see "Minutes, Steamboat Springs Planning Commission, July 1980," and a letter from Combs dated August 12, 1983. Steamboat Springs Planning. But in a personal interview in July 2011, Combs claimed that he had no intention of developing more than his own subdivision.

17 In 1959 Bill Hill went to the University of Oklahoma in Norman as assistant director for the University of Oklahoma Foundation, again as a fundraiser specializing in deferred giving programs and grant development. In 1961 he became executive director for the H.L. Snyder Research Foundation in Winfield, Kansas, and raised money for a new hospital there. In 1965 he moved to Wichita and became executive director for development at Wesley Medical Center, again focusing on public relations and fundraising. In 1970 he moved to Littleton, Colorado, and founded the Grant Development Institute. That project must have failed because 1973 found him at Bemidji State College in Minnesota as director of planning and development. In his Christmas letters from Bemidji, Hill was upbeat, as usual making lemonade out of lemons, but in fact Bemidji was at the dismal end of the planet, or nearly so. He was back in Colorado in 1975 working for Swedish Medical Center. Biographical information from Barbara Hill and Bill Hill in their book, *Our Slightly Used Studebaker* (Montrose, Colorado: 2009).

18 "Memo from William Rust to Bill Hill, April 24, 1979." CMC Archives. Rust even gave Hill a detailed "Proposed Pay-Out Schedule."

19 "United States International University, Colorado Lease Payment Schedule, January 31, 1979." CMC Archive. Hill had to acknowledge that while there was $437,000 due for bond interest, the Central Bank of Denver had only $300,000, but he was cheerfully optimistic that the payments would be made.

20 Bill Hill goes into more detail in his chapter in Lucy Bogue's book, *Miracle on a Mountain*. The bill was defeated by one vote because a senator was called out of the room and the chairman, who opposed the bill, then called for a vote that ended in a tie and (by *Robert's Rules of Order*) defeated the bill. However, it must have been clear to everyone who studied the figures that neither Steamboat Springs nor Routt County was financially strong enough to pay off bonds and finance a college, so one would have to theorize that being "called out of the room" was a prearranged tactic. In February 1980 the Colorado Commission on Higher Education voted 7-1 against a community college in Routt County.

21 Comprising both Routt and Moffat counties, this college would have included the entire Yampa River Basin from its origins in the Flattop Mountains to the Green River at the Colorado border. It made ecological but not political sense.

22 Bogue, *Miracle*, p. 147.

23 In January 1980 John Fetcher went with State Senator Richard Soash to meet with Governor Richard Lamm to ask him to place a Routt County Community College on the special legislative agenda. The real hero was Bob Adams—who owned coal mines in Routt County—and put up $75,000 to pay the money required by the bonds.

24 The campaign in Steamboat Springs, led by Bill Hill, emphasized the benefits that a college would have for the community but did not mention that the tax money would be used to pay off the interest and principal of the bondholders of 1966. The vote was extremely close in Leadville and Glenwood Springs. Glenwood Springs had a large number of conservative voters who were against any kind of property taxes for the college. During the campaign, Rex Peilstick, who headed the Yampa Valley Foundation and was an ex-officio member of the Colorado Mountain College board of trustees, was physically threatened by an irate taxpayer at a meeting in Glenwood Springs. "Personal interview with George Bagwell, November 2012."

25 Book 553, Page 471. Routt County Clerk.

26 In 1984 the lease and bond documents were amended. The Yampa Valley College Bond Authority was still identified as the landlord of the small tract; Colorado Mountain College was identified as successor to Yampa Valley College, and CMC was identified as successor to the 1969 lease and options purchase between United States International University and the Steamboat Springs school district. "Special Warranty Deed." Book 608, Page 1310, July 31, 1985. Routt County Clerk.

Chapter Six: Harvard on the Yampa

1 This caused the other two campuses to change their names: the East Campus to Timberline Campus and the West Campus to Spring Valley Campus.

2 "Personal email from Barbara Hill, July 2011." She wrote, "I would say that his views of education were more on the practical side."

3 "Personal interview with George Bagwell, July 2011."

4 Bagwell inherited a staff that had been left over from the Colorado Northwest Community College outreach center. Erie Johnson, the director of the center, was immediately replaced. But Olive Morton, Johnson's competent secretary, became interim dean of the campus and then became community education director. In 1995 she received a master's degree from Regis University. Other holdovers from the early days were Susan Good, an emergency medical technician instructor, and Denise Roach, who became executive secretary to the administration. "Bagwell interview."

5 One of the reasons Bagwell was able to do this was because F. Dean Lillie butted heads with the Colorado Mountain College trustees over finances and left the college. As a result, for a time there was weak leadership at the district office. Alpine Campus educated in three roughly equal programs: liberal arts (led by George Tolles), ski business and resort management (led by Bill Hill), and community outreach (led by Olive Morton). "Bagwell interview."

6 Bogue, *Miracle*, p. 153.

7 The cheap, prefab buildings that somewhat resembled the Lincoln Jones buildings quickly disintegrated, but left a prejudice against the buildings in Steamboat Springs.

8 Bagwell also had to fight for a campus library—the district office thought that students could use the public library.

9 Biographical material from "Tolles interview."

10 On a vacation to Austria, he met his future wife Marian.

11 This was the same advice that I had heard at Stanford University in the early 1960s when the president of the university, J. Wallace Sterling, said that he tried to hire the best teachers " . . . and then leave them alone."

12 He also learned how to dowse for Indian graves and to dowse the human body for bone and muscle problems. New Stone Age peoples believed that the earth and everything in it contained living energy. The modern conversation about energy lines began in the 1920s in England when a man named Alfred Watkins claimed that there was a system of old straight lines crisscrossing England; he called them "ley lines." His ideas were then taken up by English dowsers such as Guy Underwood and Thomas Lethbridge. Their writings became known in America in the 1960s. See Colin Wilson, *Mysteries: An Investigation into the Occult, the Paranormal, and the Supernatural* (London: Watkins Press,1978, 1999), pp. 119-136. These ideas are closely related to the Chinese ideas of Feng Shui.

13 "Personal interview with John Vickery, January 12, 2011." In the 1990s I watched as Tolles moved a negative energy line that was going through an office in Bristol Hall where the occupant was always sick. When Tolles located the energy lines for my new house in 1995, he said, "Make sure that no strong energy lines go through your bedroom; you won't get any sleep."

14 George Bagwell, a committed scientist, always shook his head and laughed when I talked with him about Tolles' dowsing. Slavoj Zizek tells the story of the physicist Neils Bohr, when a friend asked him if he believed that a horseshoe above his door would bring him good luck. "Of course not, but I've been told it works even if one doesn't believe in it." In *Less Than Nothing* (New York: Verso, 2012), p. 44.

15 In 1980 the Rockefeller Foundation published "The Humanities in American Life," the study by a commission chaired by Stanford University President Richard Lyman. It emphasized the linkage between the humanities and civic life, and also noted that knowledge of the humanities cultivated the "sanctuary of the inner life," an "interior zone of secrecy and inner experience untouched by the external world." From Harpham, *Humanities*, pp. 172-173.

16 See Paul Goodman, *Compulsory Mis-education and The Community of Scholars* (New York: Vintage Books, 1962). Goodman was an anarchist educational writer who had a strong influence on me.

17 Hadden attended the University of Colorado and then received a master's degree from Leheigh University. He later earned a doctorate from the University of Northern Colorado and became a specialist in unique and innovative methods of assessment. He became discouraged by the lack of support from the district office, and became dean of instruction at Berkeley (California) Community College, where a building was named for him after he died. His favorite system was based on the taxonomy of Benjamin Bloom (1956) that began with knowledge and moved to comprehension, application, and finally analysis.

18 Biagi is now a successful artist in Santa Fe.

19 John R. Ehrenfeld and Andrew J. Hoffmann, *Flourishing: A Frank Conversation About Sustainability* (Stanford, California: Stanford University Press, 2013), p. 113

20 See Richard Louv, *Last Child in the Woods: Saving Our Children from Nature-Deficit Disorder* (New York: Algonquin Books, 2008), p. 72.

21 Maegan Carney, a student at Colorado Mountain College from 1988 to 1990; earned a bachelor's degree with philosophy honors at the University of Colorado, Boulder; a master's degree in psychology at Naropa University; and was two-time world champion in extreme skiing, 2001-2002. See interview in the *Magazine of the Colorado Mountain College Foundation*, March 2013.

22 "Tolles interview."

Chapter Seven: Bristol Hall

1 Rick Avery then retired and was replaced by Mike Sawyer. However, there was a several month "gap" between the time Avery retired and Sawyer was hired, and this allowed a measure of autonomy for Alpine Campus.

2 Nora Richter Greer, (ed.), *AndersonMasonDale Architects* (Washington, D.C.: Grayson Publishing, 2001), p. 32.

3 "Personal interview with Paul Hack, February 3, 2011." and Greer, *AndersonMasonDale*, p. 202.

4 Greer, *AndersonMasonDale*, p. 9.

5 "Hack interview."

6 "Colorado Mountain College Alpine Campus Plan" document. Steamboat Springs Planning.

7 "CMC Alpine Campus Plan," p. 13. The Yampa River flows into Steamboat Springs from the north, and then turns west, so the town changes from a north-south orientation to an east-west one.

8 Greer, *AndersonMasonDale*, p. 114.

9 "CMC Alpine Campus Plan," p. 13.

10 I argued that the administration should move into them and move the ground-floor classrooms to the front of the building with the mountain views, but that suggestion was vigorously resisted by the administrative staff.

11 During this time, the entire Colorado Mountain College system was going through a reorganization and reappraisal due to a downturn in the district's economy. A committee, bizarrely called "R2D2," was formed to reevaluate the three residential sites of the college, and that committee decided that there could be only one residential site. Until that site was decided, Bill Gauthier again suggested that the construction on Woodchuck Hill be mothballed. John Vickery went into crisis mode. He showed how expensive it would be to stop construction. Finally "R2D2" decided that Alpine Campus would be the residential site and construction resumed. Later it was decided that the residential campuses at Alpine, Timberline, and Spring Valley would all continue. (I was personally involved with these discussions.) "Bagwell interview, July 2011."

12 *Steamboat Pilot*, December 6, 1991.

13 A comment made to me by local historic preservationist in May 2012.

14 "Personal interview with John Vickery, January 12, 2011." Vickery now thinks that he could have handled public relations in a more skillful manner.

15 "Personal interview with John Vickery, August 8, 2014."

16 *Steamboat Pilot*, March 19, 1992.

17 *Steamboat Pilot*, May 7, 1992.

18 John Vickery always took building custodian Willard Anderson to meetings with AMD, and Anderson from the beginning argued with Paul Hack about the roof. "Vickery interview."

19 "Personal interview with Brian Hoza, April 16, 2012." Colorado Mountain College sued the contractor for many mistakes in the building. The president of the college, Cynthia Heelan, bragged that the building was put up without taxpayer money because of a bond issue that the college paid off; however, in the internal budgeting of Colorado Mountain College, Alpine Campus for many years paid for that expense, now paid off.

20 "Hoza interview."

Chapter Eight: *The Academic Center*

1 The idea of calling the heads of Colorado Mountain College branches "CEO's" started with President Bob Spuhler, but such a blatant echo of the capitalist world proved to be embarrassing and was dropped in 2012.

2 "Personal interview with Peter Perhac, November 30, 2011."

3 "Personal interview with Ms. Harry Dike, July 11, 2011." Dike had come into possession of the several acres of land at the base of Woodchuck Hill originally given to Jim Temple by Steamboat Springs in the 1960s. Temple sold the land in 1961; in 1965 it was sold to Clarence Cary and became an A&W Drive-In; then Cary's Drive-In. Cary sold the business to Gary Smith, and Smith called it the Burger Express. The Dike's took over the Burger Express in 1978 and bought the land in 1981.

4 There was another problem. The access road through the Dike property, because of the configuration of Woodchuck Hill, would have to cut through a corner of the property where the city-owned Iron Spring is located. City council, over the strong objection of member Meg Bentley and historic preservation leader Jayne Hill, passed a motion to have the city "consider" condemnation action of a small part of the Iron Spring land.

5 "Minutes, City Council, City of Steamboat Springs, Colorado, September 7, 2010." Steamboat Springs Clerk.

6 "Dike interview." This was not put into the minutes, but was witnessed by Ms. Harry Dike.

7 "Dike interview."

8 "Perhac interview."

9 Shalee Cunningham, the elected trustee for CMC from Steamboat Springs, told me in a December 2011 interview that Jensen and Perhac were not serious. However, Skramstad later wrote, ". . . if we decided to pull the plug, the campus would take on a more traditional look. Just academic buildings, no dorms or support buildings. I don't think we really wanted to do that, but I think they [Stan Jensen and Peter Perhac] would have if pushed." "Personal email from Sam Skramstad, January 9, 2012."

10 The Crawford Spur road required 4,000 cubic yards of fill and cost the college an additional $3 million to build, and it created an awkward left turn.

11 "CMC correspondence, 2010." Steamboat Springs Planning.

12 This comment was not in the minutes of the city council, but was reported to me by Ms. Harry Dike, who was present at the meeting. "Dike Interviews."

13 "Minutes, City Council, City of Steamboat Springs, Colorado, January 6, 2011." Steamboat Springs Clerk.

14 In 1992 Colorado voters passed the "Taxpayer Bill of Rights," known as the TABOR amendment to the state constitution. It restricted revenue for all levels of government to rates of inflation and population and had a "ratchet-down" provision that did not allow revenues to return to higher levels after an economic recession. For entities such as Colorado Mountain College that

depended heavily on property tax revenues, it was the kiss of death for expansion. However, TABOR did allow governmental entities to go to the voters for tax increases, called "de-Brucing" after TABOR's sponsor, Douglas Bruce. In the late 1990s Cynthia Heelan, president of CMC, began a campaign to "de-Bruce" the college, and in September 2000 the voters in the college district approved TABOR relief. CMC was then able to take advantage of rising property values in its district that increased the college's mill levy revenue.

15 George Bagwell papers.

16 "Perhac interview."

17 "Personal email from Chad Novak, January 8, 2013."

18 "Minutes, City of Steamboat Springs Planning Commission, February 24, 2011." Steamboat Springs Planning.

19 "Personal email from Ariel Madlambayan of H+L Architects, January 8, 2015."

20 I attended several of these meetings, and was impressed with the efficiency and knowledge of Peter Perhac.

21 "Personal email from Debra Crawford of the CMC district office, March 5, 2014." This figure includes both the building and the access roads, but it is not clear if it includes donations.

22 "Madlambayan email."

23 During construction, Greg Hughey of High Drama Productions took many photographs of the progress and put them on a website. The ability we have in the twenty-first century to document everything with numerous digital photos—more than anyone could possible digest—has been dubbed by the *New York Times* with the neologism, hystoria, meaning to obsessively document something. See the *New York Times Magazine*, December 12, 2012. After construction was completed, the website was taken down. Historians wonder what will happen to this information in the long future: will it be erased or will it be in an unusable format?

24 In the old-fashioned days, the bookstore was a place where the faculty could see what other faculty members were ordering for their classes and discuss choices. Now books are bought online and there is no dialogue.

25 There is already at Colorado Mountain College a well-established culinary program at the Vail center.

26 See *Steamboat Pilot*, October 28, 2012. The *Steamboat Pilot* printed an article that said $2 million had been raised.

27 Chad Hanson, "Engaging Edifices," *Chronicle of Higher Education Review*, March 10, 2012.

Chapter Nine: A Minority of One

1 Of course, the CMC board of trustees could fire the president.

2 On four separate occasions I pleaded with Peter Perhac to save one of the Lincoln Jones buildings.

3 "Minutes, Faculty Senate Meeting, Alpine Campus, November 17, 2011." Copy in Robert P. Baker personal files.

4 "Personal email from Sara Lara, January 9, 2013."

5 "Personal interview with Steamboat Springs Health and Recreation Club Director Pat Carney, October 18, 2012."

6 Other items in the Willett Hall ROM are equally suspect and every item is exaggerated. There is a $20,000 estimate for "assessment" and a $50,000 estimate for "historic preservation." In fact, the college never considered a historic structure assessment and could have easily received a grant from the Colorado State Historical Fund for that purpose. Another item is "Additional Parking Lot" for $250,000. Since the space of Willett Hall was going to be used for a parking lot, the cost of keeping the building then became the cost for a new parking lot somewhere else on the campus, even though no studies had been done to see where an alternative parking lot could be located or how much it would cost. For the cost of the demolition, Debra Crawford of the CMC district office gave me a figure of $469,012. "Crawford email."

7 "Lara email."

8 Robin Pogrebin, "Architecture's Ugly Ducklings May Not Get Time to Be Swans," *New York Times*, April 7, 2012.

9 Roger Scruton, "Saving the City," *American Spectator*, 41 (October, 2008), p. 1.

10 Martin Filler, "Smash It: Who Cares?" *New York Review of Books*, November 12, 2012, p. 24.

11 Barry Munitz, "Place and History Matter on All Campuses," *Chronicle of Higher Education*, Vol. 51, No. 9, October 22, 2004.

12 Thomas Fisher, *Ethics for Architects* (New York: Princeton Architectural Press, 2010), p. 141. "The real issue, however, has to do with ethics, with the debt we owe to those before us and obligations we have to those who follow us."

13 "Personal email from George Bagwell, February 13, 2012."

14 Lutz Koepnick, *On Slowness: Toward an Aesthetic of the Contemporary* (New York: Columbia University Press, 2014), p. 46.

15 Koepnick, *On Slowness*, pp. 11,18.

16 "Crawford email." How this money was divided between the various people involved is not known.

17 "Novak email, January 8, 2013."

18 "Personal email from Arianthe Stettner, August 3, 2012."

19 "Personal telephone conversation with Meg Tully, May 4, 2012."

20 "Personal email from Alexis Eiland, April 19, 2012."

21 "Personal email from Arianthe Stettner, October 2012

Conclusion

1 In 2012 the CMC administration decided to eliminate the name "Alpine Campus" that Bill Hill had fought for in 1980 and renamed the campus "Steamboat Springs."

2 "Personal interview with George Bagwell, February 14, 2014." Of the approximately twenty-five liberal arts courses taught on the Steamboat Springs campus in the autumn of 2012, seventeen were taught by poorly paid adjuncts; twenty-five more were offered online. When I taught as an adjunct in the Spring Semester 2012, I was paid $2,730 for one course, which was more than the usual $2,100 because I was retired faculty.

3 See the website of the Critical Thinking Community: "Critical Thinking Development: A Stage Theory."

4 See Joseph Chilton Pearce, *The Heart—Mind Matrix* (Rochester, Vermont: Park Street Press, 2012), p. 30.

5 I first heard this expressed by the poet Robert Bly in Fort Collins in 1970.

6 Crane Brinton, *The Shaping of the Modern Mind* (New York: Mentor Paperback, 1953), pp. 247-248.

7 Mark Fisher, *Capitalist Realism: Is There No Alternative* (Washington, D.C.: Zero Books, 2009).

8 "Q & A with Arthur Levine," *New York Times Education Life Magazine*, November 4, 2012, p. 6.

9 Two recent books concerning the contemporary trend toward a culture of speed are Mark C. Taylor, *Speed Limits; Where Time Went and Why We Have So Little Left* (New Haven, Connecticut: Yale University Press, 2014), and Koepnick, *On Slowness*.

10 For example, about Stanford University, see Ken Auletts, "Get Rich U," *New Yorker*, April 30, 2012.

11 "Education Secretary: Colleges Need Grades Too," *Time*, September 20, 2013.

12 See Michael J. Sandel, *What Money Can't Buy: The Moral Limits of Markets* (New York: Farrar, Straus, and Giroux, 2012), pp. 5, 84-85. Sandel points out that academic economists have changed emphasis: in 1958 Paul Samuelson's best-selling *Economics* defined economics with its traditional subject matter (prices, wages, etc.) but today economics has to do with the language of incentives and the idea that economic incentives determine behavior to the detriment of any kind of incentives based on other values. See also Robert Skidelsky and Edward Skidelsky, *How Much Is Enough: Money and the Good Life* (New York: Other Press, 2012), and Charlie Eisenstein, *Sacred Economics: Money, Gift, and Society in the Age of Transition* (Berkeley, California: University of California Press, 2011).

Appendix 2: The Architectural Career of Lincoln Jones after 1966.

1 Whether any of Lincoln Jones' projects were ever built in the Roaring Fork Valley remains a mystery. None of the local historians or historical societies in the Roaring Fork Valley remember Jones, and he has disappeared down the memory hole there. Bob McHugh claims that Jones designed the Rifle High School that has since been enclosed by another building.

2 "Personal interview with Bill Fetcher, October 2010." Joe Robbins, an architect who worked for Lincoln Jones in his younger days, told me that he was "thankfully" happy that Jones' plans for a united Lincoln Avenue were never realized. "Del" Haute of Del's Jewelry told me that Jones tried to twist his arm to put a mansard roof on Haute's building, but Haute refused.

3 Knedler's mansard roof was removed in 2009.

4 "Carney interview."

5 The Cultural Resource Survey site form completed in 2009 for this property shows that apparently Jones planned a 1972 remodel of the house, but did not design the house, built in 1959.

6 It became known locally as the "round" house, a term Lincoln Jones disliked.

7 By the late 1990s the buildings had long been empty and neglected. The property owner, ignoring city regulations, demolished them without notice. He was fined.

8 "Lincoln Jones obituary," *Steamboat Pilot*, April 1988.

9 "Personal interview with Glen Jones, January 16, 2011."

10 Evidently it was the style for Middle East rulers to have fleets of Ferrari's. See "The Last Pharaoh and His Ferrari: An Exclusive Berlina for the Infamous Farouk," *Automobile Quarterly*, Vol. 27, No. 2 (1989), pp. 148-159.

11 There was one other Lincoln Jones' building, located in the area behind the Holiday Inn, vacant in the 1970s but now a subdivision. It was described in John T. Stone, *Going for Broke*, (New York: Regnery, 1976), p. 72. "There was only one structure on the property: a unique, mushroom-shaped house with its octagonal living quarters perched atop a central pedestal." I can find neither pictures nor plans for this house.

12 I have been unable to find a photograph of this building.

Index